DOLLS' HOUSES

DOLLS' HOUSES

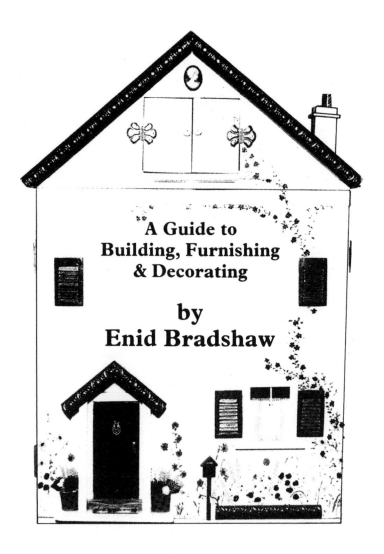

A Guide to
Building, Furnishing
& Decorating

by
Enid Bradshaw

BLANDFORD PRESS
POOLE • NEW YORK • SYDNEY

First published in the UK 1986 by Blandford Press
Link House, West Street, Poole, Dorset BH15 1LL

World Copyright © John Ferguson (Pty) Ltd, Publishers

Distributed in the United States by
Sterling Publishing Co, Inc,
2 Park Avenue, New York, NY 10016

British Library Cataloguing in Publication Data

Bradshaw, Edna
  Doll's houses : building, furnishing, decorating.
  1. Doll's houses
  I. Title
  745.592'3   TT175.3

ISBN 0 7137 1913 3

Typeset by Post Typesetters
Printed in Hong Kong

Table of Contents

Introduction 1

Selecting a Dollhouse 2

Building a Dollhouse 4
Materials 4
Design and Construction 4
Stairs 7
Painting and Decorating 9
Windows and Doors 10
Adornments 12

Interior Decorating 13
Choice of Colours 13
Wallpapers 13
Floor Coverings 13
Light Fittings 14
Furniture 15
Curtains 16
Manchester 16

Accessories 18
All the Little Bits and Pieces 18
Food 19

The Residents 20
Making a Miniature Doll 21

Clothing for Miniature Dolls 25
Clothes for Female Dolls 25
Clothes for Little Girl Dolls 32
Clothes for Male Dolls 32

Clothes for Little Boy Dolls 33
Socks 34
Shoes 34

Visiting the Miniature World 36
Linley Court 36
Blossom Cottage 39
The Schoolhouse 41
Rainbow Arcade 42

Making Furniture and Accessories 45
The Preliminaries 45
Basic Design for Various Items 46
Tables and Chairs 47
The Fire and Fireplace 52
Bedroom Furniture 53
Other Furniture 56
Nursery Needs 57
Accessories and Extras 60
Pots and Flowers 64
Bottles 65
Frames, Pictures and Mirrors 66
Clocks 67
Books 67
Using Pictures from Advertisements 68
Articles Made with Modelling Plastic 69
Food Made from Dough 75
Making Food from Other Materials 75

Other Ideas 77

For Catherine, Jacinta, Christopher and Damien

Introduction

Do you have a secret dreamhouse? Many of us do. They are wonderful, fanciful places that very rarely come our way in real life. Yet our dreamhouses could actually materialise, if we wish, complete to the finest detail. Elegant rooms and beautiful furniture could become ours in a miniature house. We could delight in designing, decorating and furnishing, and in filling the house with exciting accessories. It could become a showcase for collected miniature treasures, or be endowed with a life of its own with a family of miniature dolls. A miniature house, or dollhouse, inspires new interests that could develop into an absorbing and fascinating pastime.

The earliest known dollhouses came from Germany and Holland in the seventeenth century. They were usually very elaborate and not for the use of children. It was only during Victorian times that little girls generally became dollhouse owners, and furnished miniature houses became as much a part of the upper-class nursery as the dappled rocking horse.

The world's most famous dollhouses are actually miniature palaces. The best known are Queen Mary's Dollhouse and Titania's Palace. The former was built in 1924 by the most gifted artists and craftsmen in Britain and it can still be seen at Windsor Castle. Titania's Palace was made by an Irishman for his daughter as a home for Titania, the queen of the fairies. It took fifteen years to build and has everything a royal family could wish for, including a central courtyard filled with flowers and a jewelled throne in the royal chamber. Titania's Palace was taken around the world during the 1930s to show children where the fairy queen lived with Oberon the king and their little princesses. The fairy people themselves were, of course, quite invisible.

We can have lovely dollhouses, too, if we are prepared to spend a little time and effort. Today's miniature residences often include detailed copies of contemporary interiors and, although it is difficult for us to believe that one day these furnishings will be old-fashioned or quaint or antique, this is inevitable as time goes by. Many of the dollhouses that we see in museums are family heirlooms from previous centuries, and so today's dollhouses will eventually become heirlooms for our own future generations.

Any person with an aptitude for crafts could produce miniature furniture and accessories, and nobody knows whether they have that ability until they have at least tried. Perhaps this could be an undertaking in which the whole family might find a common interest, including members of the older generation who may have a store of hidden talents. Most small boys would love to participate, too, possibly by helping to build a garage for the family motor car and a service station along the 'street'. My young grandsons suggested a nearby space station for outer-space visitors! However, I doubt that itinerant Martians would be made very welcome at a conservative dollhouse.

Children, playing in their world of make-believe, can enjoy countless hours arranging and rearranging furniture. They can conduct dinner parties, go on shopping trips, care for a baby in the nursery and organise the running of a busy household with all of the pleasures of real life and none of the problems. Owning a dollhouse allows children to express suppressed emotions during their play. It also stimulates their imagination and encourages creativity.

Selecting a Dollhouse

Commercially produced dollhouses are available in a range of materials and designs. Their prices range from about $60 for the very basic to about $550 for the more sophisticated.

Plastic houses of American manufacture can be purchased at most toyshops in kit form with each part completely painted and decorated. They are most appealing, although their light construction would make them less suitable for the younger age groups.

Ready-made Australian timber dollhouses are generally of a stronger construction. They come unpainted and unadorned, thus giving the new owner scope for personal decorating and choice of colours. They are usually made of pine or marine ply and are available at toyshops specialising in quality toys.

Particle-board or pine houses in a variety of designs and sizes are also obtainable in kit form and sold by individual importers. Some of these kits are fully complete and ready for assembly. Others include the basic structure only and allow the purchaser to buy separately whatever doors, windows and trimmings are preferred.

Occasionally, superb craftsman-built miniature houses that are perfect to the smallest item, are for private sale. Unfortunately these rare offerings cost thousands of dollars and consequently are beyond the limits of most buyers.

The alternative to buying either a ready-made or kit-form house is to purchase the materials and become your own builder. Hopefully you would get exactly what you want in this way, be it an Australian colonial, a rose-covered Cotswold, an established architectural style or just a square box fitted with a door. You may make it single-storied, two-storied, or as high as you can reach! Perhaps you could make the basic structure yourself and fit it out with purchased components such as windows and doors to give it a professional finish.

The width should be considered, as the dollhouse will be part of the home furnishings, whether it is kept in a child's bedroom or in a place of honour in the living room. Allowance should also be made for the space that the opened doors will require. In the case of a very wide dollhouse it would be an advantage to make bi-folding doors if the windows can be spaced to avoid the hinged area. Ideally the dollhouse should be situated upon a shelf or low table for ease of use and viewing.

An essential feature of a dollhouse is good access to its interior. This is gained by the opening of an entire wall, either the front or back. Those that open at the back have the disadvantage of having to be turned around whenever in use, and moving the structure causes objects inside to topple over which is frustrating to say the least. The problem can be overcome by placing the house away from the wall, although this is not always practical. Front openings have no such complications and nothing is sacrificed by entering the house from the front — after all that is usually the way we approach our own home.

For very young children a dollhouse should be basic, roomy and of solid construction. Preferably it should have access from the front and have no enclosing doors. The furniture should be sturdy because fragile articles soon meet a very disappointing end. For safety's sake, do not include any glass items or very small objects. Lots of little floor mats and bedclothes could be supplied in bright colours. A family of strongly made dolls, with perhaps a pet cat or dog or something else a little different, could be provided for amusement. The conversation piece in my little grand-daughters' dollhouse is a family of well-dressed toy mice living in the attic with their own furniture and with pictures of rodent relatives hanging on the wall.

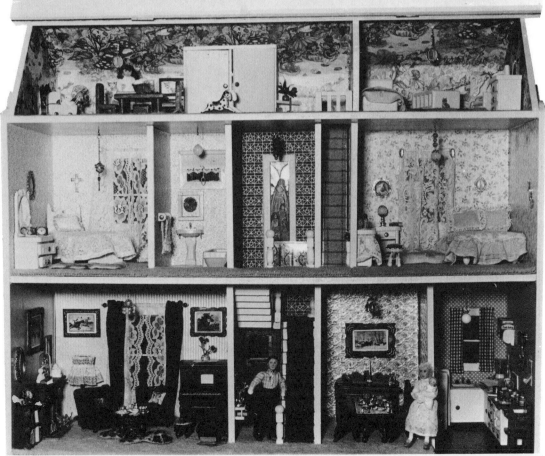

Building a Dollhouse

Materials

It is not necessary to be a tradesman to make a dollhouse, but it would be helpful to possess just a little elementary carpentry skill. You will first of all need a place where you can work with access to fresh air, remembering that many glues contain toxic fumes. Very few tools are needed. A sharp handsaw, a small coping saw, hammer, screwdriver, plyers and a drill are the major items. You will also need a supply of medium and fine sandpapers, a tape measure, plastic set square, nail punch and craft knife.

Materials can be chosen according to preference. Size 9.5 mm plywood and chipboard are the most popular for a solid construction, the latter being the more economical. If you intend to build a fairly small dwelling your timber merchant may have off-cuts sufficient for your needs. Balsa wood, obtainable from hobby shops, is excellent for window and door architraves and a wide range of thicknesses are available. If a heavier wood is preferred for the trimmings, buy some very narrow picture framing or beading. Fancy beading of different widths is very attractive and adds extra decoration to the dollhouse exterior. If you have not used balsa wood before it might help to know that it is very soft and can easily be sandpapered out of shape — or even out of existence — if it is worked on too vigorously.

Hinges depend upon the size of the doors you are making, but keep them as small and unobtrusive as possible. For use with chipboard buy self-tapping screws (or special chipboard screws if available) and make sure that they fit the hinges but are not so long that they penetrate through to the other side of the timber. Panel pins are necessary, and useful sizes are 6 mm and 12 mm.

There are many glues on the market. Any contact glue that dries fairly quickly is satisfactory. On very small areas and fine timber, use a fast-drying acetate cement that is available at hobby shops. For wallpapering and other paper and fabric work, a white glue is most suitable.

Design and Construction

It is most important to make careful plans on paper before buying any materials. Give yourself a questionnaire to answer. What style of house have you in mind? Is it for a young child, an older child or an adult? What size do you want? Have you room space to accommodate it? Do you prefer access to the dollhouse from the front or the back? Do you want part of the roof opening to the attic? What shape roof do you like: hip, gable or flat? Do you want to build the basics only and buy the doors, windows and stairs ready-made? Would you rather buy a book of plans and just follow the instructions?

The standard scale generally used in dollhouses is 25.4 mm to 304.8 mm (one inch to one foot) or 1:12. It is a good idea to work to this size as any manufactured extras or furniture you may wish to buy would most likely be in this scale.

There are no fixed rules for designs, unless you are a perfectionist. Room sizes are whatever suit you best. The lounge room, or sitting room, should be the most generous in the house, and you would have to know approximately how you intend to furnish it before deciding on its size. Basically there would be a lounge suite, occasional table and standard lamp. But there could also be a piano and stool, a fireplace, a bookcase and a television set. The main bedroom would accommodate a double bed, a dressing table, a wardrobe (unless it is built in) and possibly a bedside table and a chair. It is best to draw a floor plan of the house on a large sheet of paper, divide it into 25.4 mm (one inch) squares, each representing 304.8 mm (one foot), and cut some pieces of cardboard the approximate sizes of the expected furniture. Move the 'furniture' around on the floor plan, placing it in different positions and allowing for curtain widths across any windows in the plan, until you have a fair idea of the furniture layout and room sizes required. And then allow a bit extra because you never know what items you may wish to add to your collection later and it would be most disheartening if they could not be fitted in.

The depth of the rooms also varies but I favour approximately 304.8 mm, as rooms that are too recessed are lost in shadow. Wide, rather than deep, rooms give more space in which to move around.

Allow 355 mm for ceiling height on the ground floor as we usually look down to that level and need the height to see inside. As the house gets higher, less floor-to-ceiling space is required, say 305 mm for the first floor and 254 mm for the attic. These are approximate suggestions only.

Adjustments must be made while you are still in the planning stage. Once the timber is cut it is too expensive to change your mind, and after walls have been glued together it is almost impossible to alter them.

If you wish to make a simple dollhouse, basic units could be the answer.

A single unit measuring 406 mm wide × 380 mm high × 304 mm deep (or whatever sizes you prefer) makes one room. This can be turned into an ideal small shop or schoolroom. A pediment glued on top hides the flat roof, and a drop-down door becomes a footpath once the unit is opened (Fig. 1). To make a shop, fit the interior with a counter and several shelves.

Extend the sides and back of the single unit and add a lid, and you have a one-roomed cottage with an attic (Fig. 2). Glue artificial grass and some pot-plants inside the drop-down front and the cottage has a front garden.

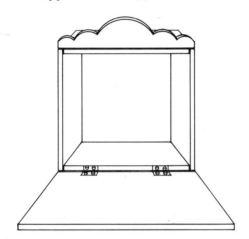

Fig. 1

Basic unit with drop-down front

Example of exterior

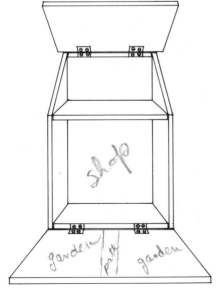

Fig. 2

Basic unit with attic

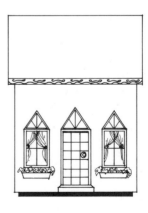

Example of exterior

5

Building one unit on top of another and including an attic results in a Victorian-style terrace house. This style requires a pair of conventional doors (Fig. 3).

By putting four units together with an attic, quite a sizable dollhouse is created (Fig. 4).

Whatever the design or size of the finished product, it would be an advantage to glue a 25 mm plinth underneath to facilitate the opening of the doors.

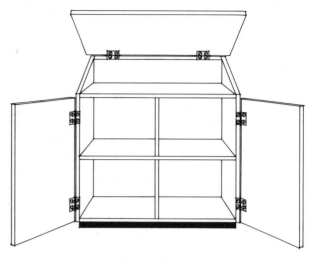

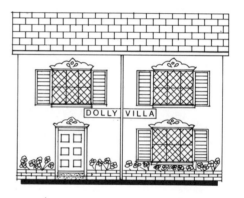

Fig. 4
Four units with attic

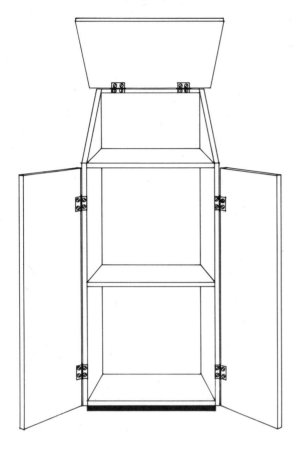

Example of exterior

Fig. 3
Two units with attic

Stairs

Stairs constitute the most difficult part of making a dollhouse, so it is better to keep the style simple. Curved stairways and landings are tempting, but even commercial dollhouses frequently have them straight. As a reasonable slope for stairs has to be accomplished in whatever space is available, it is not always possible to work to the 1:12 scale —a lapse which is usually not noticed or else is forgiven. Try to position stairs next to a wall so that they can be glued together for stability. The most practical solution to the difficulty of stair-making is to purchase them ready-made. However, two simple methods of stair construction are as follows:

1. Measure the width of the intended stairs and cut a number of blocks to that length. Use a light timber about 45 mm × 20 mm dressed. Starting at the bottom, pile the blocks upwards with one on top of the other, sloping them backwards as you go until they reach the hole that has been made in the ceiling above. Make sure that the top block meets the level correctly by moving the entire flight a little forward or backward. When satisfied that the stairs will fit, glue the blocks together (Fig. 5).

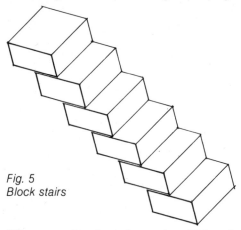

Fig. 5
Block stairs

2. Measure the length and width of the proposed stairs and cut a piece of thin balsa to that size. This is the stair support. You will also need a length of balsa 20 mm square. Cut this into lengths that measure the width of the stairs, then with a craft knife carefully slice through each of these blocks diagonally. This will result in small triangular shapes. Glue each of these, one above the other, on to the base to form neat little steps. Put the stairway into position, adjusting as in the first method (Fig. 6).

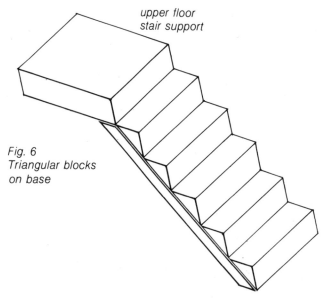

Fig. 6
Triangular blocks on base

upper floor
stair support

Bannisters and handrails are necessary to stairways. For the bannisters, use plain 3 mm dowel (available at hobby shops), plain or carved wooden toothpicks, or very fine cocktail picks. Cut them to the length required, then insert the lower end of each into a tiny block of balsa that neatly fits upon a stair. Thread a small wooden bead on to each balustrade and glue it to the wooden block at the bottom. Cut a railing of 6 mm square balsa to fit the tops of the balustrades, press the railing down and enlarge the resulting indentations with a nail. Glue the railing into position. End posts can be carved effectively from balsa, or make a post by threading and gluing wooden beads on to a wooden toothpick (Fig. 7).

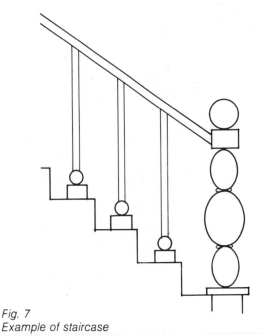

Fig. 7
Example of staircase

For a handrail that is attached to a wall, cut a length of 3 mm dowel, put a wooden bead on each end and glue the beads to the wall (Fig. 8). A more decorative handrail can be made by draping a length of jewellery chain (from a cheap necklace) in festoons and fastening it to the wall with gold upholstery pins (Fig. 9). It is important to remember that the wall must be either painted or papered before handrails are attached.

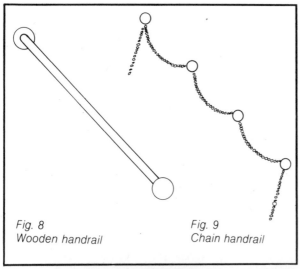

Fig. 8
Wooden handrail

Fig. 9
Chain handrail

Painting and Decorating

Always sandpaper finished work and remove the dust before undercoating and again before the final coat of paint. Any all-purpose undercoats and good quality semi-gloss paints are quite suitable. For trimmings such as shutters and architraves full-gloss enamel in 100 ml tins is best. One or two colours only should be sufficient, but for a really bright exterior it would be necessary to purchase a few more. By buying white and the three primary colours of red, blue and yellow, other colours can be made without extra cost. Save up bottle tops and jar lids in which to mix the colours as you need them, and remember always to add the stronger colour last. Yellow plus a dash of blue makes apple green; add more blue for darker green; yellow plus a dash of red makes orange; a little each of red and blue makes purple; white with a little red makes pink; and white gives a pastel version of any colour added to it.

Colour schemes are planned according to the painter's taste, but a good rule to observe is to have the main colour soft, the trimmings of a complementary colour, and small highlights of a bright contrasting colour.

As the project progresses, new ideas for additions or variations will emerge and here is where imagination comes in handy. The exterior walls might look nice with a brickwork appearance. To achieve this (after the final coat of paint has thoroughly dried) mark out a pattern of brickwork over the entire area except where any painted windows or doors or special features are to be placed. Use a ruler and a fine brown or black felt-tipped pen. An ordinary ball-point pen is not satisfactory (Fig. 10).

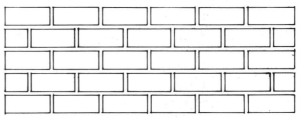

Fig. 10
Brick design

A tiled roof can be ruled out in the same way, substituting a tile pattern for the brick. An impressive shingle roof is easily made by using scissors to cut shingles from 1.6 mm balsa and gluing them on to the roof in overlapping rows. However, when attaching shingles, the roof should not have been previously painted. If it has been painted it will need sanding very well before applying the glue. A narrow ridge-capping would provide a pleasing finish to a shingled roof. It can be made of balsa, with the edges cut into scallops (Fig. 11).

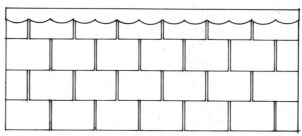

Fig. 11
Shingle tile pattern

Paint all the ceilings before assembling the house. It will save you standing on your head to do it later.

Windows and Doors

Windows and doors do not have to be cut out, as painted versions are an interesting alternative. If, however, you are cutting them out, do so before the walls are put together. This rule also applies to doors connecting rooms in interior walls.

Cut-out Window

Cut some very thin clear perspex a little larger than the window space. Glue it into place on the inside of the window, taking care not to get glue on the plastic. Make the architraves for both the inside and the outside of the window. Use a small mitre box for making the architraves, or cut them with neat square corners. Keep the inside architrave simple but the outside may be as simple or ornate as you wish. An ornamental cornice or moulding along the top is attractive. With a match-thin piece of 4.8 mm balsa, make a horizontal window strut. Paint all the woodwork before gluing it into place (Fig. 12).

If you have difficulty in obtaining suitable plastic for the window, real glass can be used, unless of course the dollhouse is to be used by young children. If square or diamond panes are preferred, use opaque adhesive tape cut into very thin strips to form the pattern.

Fig. 12
Cut-out window with shutters

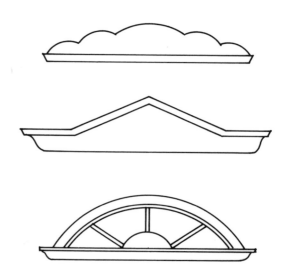

Examples of ornamental cornices

Cut-out Door

Cut a piece of timber the same thickness as the wall to form the door. Fit it loosely in the doorway, allowing space for the thickness of the paint, and with a sufficient gap at the bottom to clear whatever floor covering is to be used in the house where the door is to open. Decorate and paint the door and attach it to the opening with the smallest suitable hinges. Add the architrave and a cornice if required (Fig. 13a). There are many door styles from which to choose:

Panelled: Cut out small oblongs or squares of 1.6 mm balsa and glue them onto the door in whatever design suits you. When the glue is dry, apply undercoat to the door and panelling. When that is dry, sandpaper the panelling lightly until smooth before applying the final coat of paint (Fig. 13b).

Tongued and grooved: With a coping saw or sharp knife score the door in vertical lines before painting it (Fig. 13c).

Glazed or half-glazed: Cut whatever shape is required out of the door. Paint it and allow to dry. On the inside of the cut-out area glue plastic or glass that has been cut a little larger than the hole (Fig. 13d).

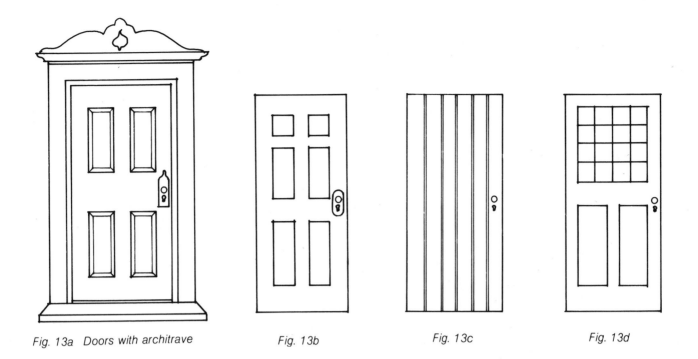

Fig. 13a Doors with architrave   Fig. 13b   Fig. 13c   Fig. 13d

Painted-on Door

Draw an outline of the door in the correct position on the wall of the house. Cut a door the same size as the outline from a piece of 1.6 mm balsa. Decorate this in the same way as for the cut-out door. When completed and painted, glue the door onto the drawn outline. Add the architrave.

Painted-on Window

Although achieving a painted window is not difficult, it would be a good idea to experiment on a piece of previously painted timber before attempting work on the project itself. Draw an outline of the required window on its allotted space. Dilute brown oil paint with a little turpentine. Working quickly because the paint must not dry out, brush the brown over the window area. With a small crumpled piece of stiff lace or rough fabric 'draw' curtains by dragging the fabric gently across the surface of the paint, working towards you (Fig. 14a). By guiding the fabric, a pattern can be formed to represent straight hanging curtains or a cross-over style. Still working quickly, use the point of a toothpick and scratch in any small details such as a pattern in the curtain material or frilly edges. Allow to dry thoroughly.

If a blind is to be included in the window, paint it after the curtains have been painted. While it is still wet, scratch out a fringe along the bottom.

Paint on a blind pull with a fine brush. Let it dry well. If any paint has strayed on to the wall area during the painting of the window, wipe it off with a rag slightly dampened with turpentine.

Make and paint the architrave and window strut and, when dry, glue them into position (Fig. 14b).

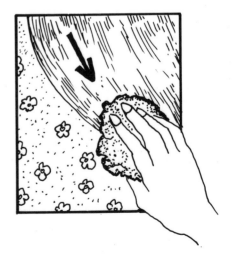

Fig. 14a
Painted-on window

Window Shutters

Shutters are bright additions to a house and can be made from 4.8 mm balsa. Lightly score them horizontally to suggest louvres and either paint or stain them. If the louvres need to be emphasised, simply go over them with a fine black or brown felt-tipped pen after the paint has dried (Figs 12 and 14b).

Fig. 14b
Example of completed painted-on window

Adornments

Now we come to fun-time when we can add all the adornments. Here are some suggestions:
— Add a painted keyplate and keyhole to the front door and press in a small gold pin for a knob, or else attach a purchased brass keyplate.
— Add a front door knocker (dangling parts of old earrings are ideal) or else put a bell-push on the side architrave by pushing a plastic-headed pin through a chromed collar washer.
— Paint black decorative strap hinges on the door, or cut them out of black paper or cardboard and glue them on.
— Make a 'stained glass' fanlight over the door from coloured pieces of plastic or glass.
— Put a small porch around the door just wide enough for a door mat and an ornamental tub of flowers.
— Make a little letterbox of balsa, paint it a bright colour and glue it to the front wall near the door.
— Add a weathercock to the roof, or a dovecote, or a chimney-pot (provided of course that there is a fireplace in the house).

— Paint a garden of colourful flowers against the front wall, or a vine creeping around the windows. If you haven't sufficient confidence in your painting, cut out some tiny pictures of plants and glue them on.
— Make balsa wood window-boxes and fill them with artificial flowers and trailing ivy. Do not use dried flowers because they will deteriorate in time.

Of course the house must have a name! Decide on the name and cut a piece of 1.6 mm balsa of a suitable length. Paint and sandpaper it, then print or stencil the title on and glue the name plate to the house. Surround it with a small frame of beading. You may have some interesting ideas of your own for making the name-plate, especially if you are handy with plastics or copper.

You will probably continue to dream up other decorations as you advance. Do not hesitate to add them. Dollhouses cannot be overdressed, as part-realism, part-fantasy is their enchantment. They require caution only in keeping as close as possible to the scale of 1:12. For instance, do not be tempted into using any artificial flowers that are too large, as they would throw everything else out of proportion. Search long enough and the right size can eventually be found.

The finishing touches are the personal signature to your work. Applying your own ideas gives your dollhouse individuality — something that cannot be obtained other than through your own efforts. It may be time-consuming work, but when it is finished you will have created something original — and that is quite an achievement.

Finally, add a small unobtrusive catch of some kind on the enclosing doors. The house is now ready for the interior decorators.

Interior Decorating

Choice of Colours

First of all, look at the overall interior and give some thought to a unifying colour scheme. Never consider just one room at a time as a patchy effect could result. Ideally a consistent basic colour should link each room. The floor coverings are usually best qualified to accomplish this. Decide whether one colour should dominate or whether variations on a theme would look better. Complementary colours can be added in scatter rugs, bedspreads and curtains. Experiment with contrasting and strong colours in small items only. The colours within each room, however, should be in harmony. For example, if the wallpaper in the bedroom is green floral, use a plain matching green for the bedspread and perhaps the side drapes of the curtains. White could be the colour of the centre lace curtain and of one or two floor mats. Elegant highlights could be gold frames of pictures and mirror and perhaps a gilded vanity stool. Colours should be attuned to the nature of the room — black and silver would be dramatic in a formal dining room but would be most unsuitable for a child's bedroom; and where bright red or green would light up a kitchen, a chintzy sitting room would be ruined.

Wallpapers

For the sake of not damaging the floor coverings it is better to do the wallpapering first. Real wallpapers are sometimes acceptable, but can be a little clumsy and few of them have sufficiently small patterns. Dollhouse wallpapers are available at some hobby shops, although these are comparatively expensive. Good quality gift-wrapping papers from stationery shops are usually successful and often have lovely patterns suitable for dollhouse needs, especially miniature spots and florals. Stripes in various colours are timeless and classy, but if the stripes are too far apart they create a cage-like effect in a small room. Embossed foil looks superb with a setting of dark furniture and is worth the extra care needed in its handling. The main points to remember are to avoid large or overpowering patterns and to beware of cheap quality papers which are very likely to fade.

Do one wall at a time. Cut the paper to fit exactly and allow an overlap to run around each corner to ensure that there is no gap between joins. In other words, wallpaper a dollhouse the same way that you wallpaper your own home. Lay the cut paper face down on a clean surface and cover it rapidly with a fairly liberal amount of white glue. Apply the paper to the wall, working quickly, smoothing gently with a damp rag until it is in the correct position and has no creases. If any glue gets on to the surface of the paper, wet it with a little water and pat it with a damp rag. Do not rub hard or you will have a nicely papered wall with a hole in it. If such a catastrophe does occur, just cut out a piece from the scraps of wallpaper, carefully match the pattern and make sure it is large enough to fit over the hole, then glue it on. Properly done it cannot be detected.

Floor Coverings

Coverings for floors take a priority in interior decorating. Carpets contribute colour, texture, comfort and a feeling of luxury, and are therefore very popular. Real carpet is usually too thick for dollhouses and causes the tiny furniture to fall over. Special dollhouse plush floor covering is excellent but is not always available. Some good quality upholstery fabrics serve beautifully, especially those with a touch of velvet in them. Be wary of over-patterned materials.

Anybody with a small weaving loom or a talent for needlepoint has a wonderful opportunity to manufacture perfect carpets and rugs.

The following anecdote illustrates the enthusiasm people often develop for their hobby. I was speaking to an ardent collector of miniatures and he confided that he had been given an expensive woven necktie by a friend recently returned from a trip to Germany. He immediately saw its possibilities and unpicked it (presumably after his benefactor had gone), cut it into a rectangle, blanket-stitched the edges, and happily placed the heirloom-worthy rug into his miniature lounge room!

For those who do not receive such gifts, plain felt is available in many colours in craft shops. Most importantly, it can be patterned with fabric paints to your own design, and without too much effort a room-sized square can be transformed into an Axminster carpet. White felt, if painted with pastel colours and with a fringe stitched around it, becomes a Numdah rug. Felt rugs can be cut into any shape and do not unravel. They can be embroidered or appliqued and lend themselves particularly to oriental designs.

Many quality floor coverings can be made from discarded tapestry samples, woollen scarves, tweed, chenille, velvet and fur fabrics. If the pile of fur fabric is too deep, it only requires a haircut with scissors. Left-over knitting wools can be crocheted into oval or round mats that look very pretty with a tassel fringe.

If room-sized carpets are to be glued to the floor, use just a smear of white glue. Smooth the surface perfectly flat, making sure that the fabric is not being stretched. Should there be any doubt that the material might shrink, weigh it down evenly until the glue has dried.

Shiny-surfaced wallpapers or plastic contact papers with a tile, marble or cork pattern are suitable for kitchen or bathroom floors.

Floors may be covered with purchased parquet or miniature floorboarding on ready-to-lay self-adhesive backing. Alternatively, they need not be covered at all, but stained or painted and highly varnished for a good effect. There are plenty of options.

Light Fittings

Every room must have an overhead light fitting and some rooms should have a standard or table lamp as well. These add up to quite a few lights. All are obtainable commercially, and are usually electrically activated by three-volt batteries housed in small plastic boxes. Each battery supplies three lights and, if a miniature transformer is employed, six or more lights can be connected. If you are uncertain about the placing of the lights it would be a good idea to draw a plan of the dollhouse showing where lights are required and take it to a hobby shop for personal advice.

Some dollhouses are wired for real lighting. If this is being considered, allowances should be made for the wiring when the house is being constructed. The wiring itself is not difficult but the power supply presents a problem. Either a transformer or batteries are required, depending upon the system chosen, but both are difficult to accommodate discreetly in the miniature house unless perhaps space could be spared in the attic. Plans for wiring are available in specialist books, but expert advice should be sought in this matter.

If your dollhouse does not employ electricity, it is a very simple matter to manufacture your own imitation light fittings. These can be made from bright glass beads about 20 mm diameter, or from small beads or crystal drops wired in clusters to form chandeliers. They can hang from lengths of necklace chain attached to the ceiling with small eye screws (Fig. 15a). A table lamp can be made

Fig. 15a
Ceiling lights

14

from a large glass bead glued on an upright of 3 mm dowel inserted into a wooden base. An alternative upright could be a toothpick threaded with wooden or glass beads or brass dress eyelets (Fig. 15b).

The upright for a standard lamp could be made of wooden beads threaded on rigid wire. If the base of a standing lamp cannot support the superstructure, glue a flat metal washer underneath, or use a chromed nut instead of a wooden base (Fig. 15c). A shade for a standard lamp is easily made from part of a cardboard cylinder from the centre of plastic wrap, covered with fabric (Fig. 15d).

Table and standard lamps

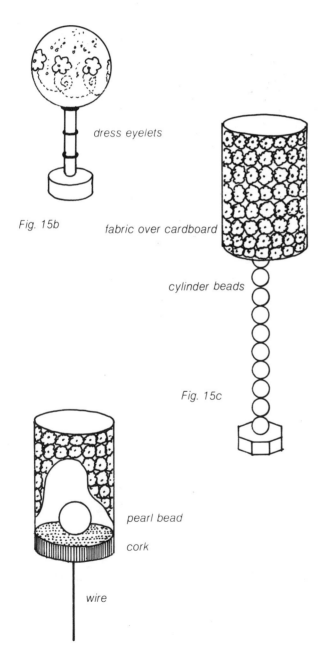

dress eyelets

Fig. 15b

fabric over cardboard

cylinder beads

Fig. 15c

pearl bead

cork

wire

Fig. 15d

A period-style house would not have light fittings at all, but should be supplied with oil lamps and candles. Extra light can be admitted to the house by having cut-out windows in the back wall of each room. Even when covered with lace drapes they let in light if the dollhouse stands against a window. For a special effect, an ordinary electric light globe or small table lamp can be rigged up behind the dollhouse to flood the rooms with what appears to be sunshine.

Furniture

If you are striving for realism in your dollhouse do not be enticed by cheap plastic furniture. However, there are two exceptions, the bathroom and the kitchen, for which plastic furniture, especially the stronger types from West Germany and England, are well suited. These items are very attractive and usually include luxury items such as dishwashing machines and shower recesses. Alternatives for the bathroom are simple ceramic settings and, for older-style houses, Victorian settings with mahogany trimming and a high price tag. Colonial settings in pine finish are obtainable for the kitchen, and there are a few very attractive modern designs made of wood combined with a little plastic.

Timber furniture for bedrooms, dining rooms and living rooms offers a wide range from which to choose in antique, contemporary or colonial designs, and most of these items are of good quality. The variety is endless and there is scarcely an article normally found in the home that has not been reproduced. Today, with imports from Taiwan, some pieces cost as little as two or three dollars each. Of course top quality crafted work could cost up to ten times as much.

The pleasure in owning a dollhouse can be even greater if you have created the furniture yourself. It is quite impossible to put a price on the effort and time involved in making furniture as a hobby, but it is a pastime that offers a most satisfying method of self-expression.

As there are very few suitable softwoods in Australia, choosing the right one is not a big problem! Tasmanian huon pine is perhaps the best, although extremely expensive and not easily obtainable. Radiata pine is acceptable but the occasional knots in the grain have to be avoided when using it for miniature work. Pacific maple does not offer too many problems, and cedar is also highly suitable, although more costly. Beech, mostly imported from America, was used very successfully in the past but it is now practically impossible to buy. I realised this fact with both chagrin and amusement when I once asked a timber merchant if he had any dressed beech for sale. He said he knew of a man who knew of another man who had a property somewhere up in the far north, and this man had a beech tree that he might consider selling for a couple of thousand dollars, if I went up there! As I wanted neither a whole tree nor a trip to somewhere in the far north, I settled instead for a short length of cedar. Walnut and mahogany are beautiful timbers favoured by craftsmen who are fortunate enough to possess the specialised power tools necessary for working hardwoods in miniature. Of the materials readily available for our purposes, however, balsa wood seems to be the best. Furthermore, it is easily obtainable in many sizes and shapes from hobby shops. When a little extra weight is required (for perhaps a table or bed) Pacific maple provides the answer.

Using balsa wood or a mixture of timbers has complications when it comes to the finishing process. These can be overcome by using an antique paint (base, colour and varnish) which comes in all timber colours and gives a very pleasing finish.

It is advisable to keep to a simple furniture design at first. As you progress you will want to do more intricate work, especially antique styles, and this will not be difficult if you use a real piece of furniture or a photograph to guide you. You will be pleasantly surprised at how successful the results will be. The instructions for making some furniture items are included in the final chapter of this book.

Curtains

Dominant or clumsily made curtains can spoil the balance of a room. It is important to choose fabrics that will fall softly and hang close to the wall. Usually very lightweight materials such as lace, silk, dacron and voile are best, although some of the heavier fabrics such as knits and velvet hang equally well, so each must be judged on its merits. Sometimes stiff or rebellious fabrics need to be guided into neat drapes, and there are many ways to achieve this. Here are two worth trying:

1. Cut finely corrugated cardboard to the required size, brush it thinly with white glue and gently press the material into the corrugations. Fold a little material under at the top, bottom and sides to form hems.

2. Cut a piece of aluminium foil about twice the width the curtain is to be when completed. Brush thinly with white glue and press the fabric on flat. Allow to dry thoroughly. Turn under the hems, then fold the foil up concertina-wise. Open up the newly formed pleats and the curtain is finished.

For softly draped cross-over curtains, make a tie-back of some matching embroidery cotton.

Attach curtain tops to a rod of 3 mm dowel. It is acceptable to fold the fabric over the rod and glue it, otherwise a fine hem can be stitched and the rod inserted through it. If the glue method is used, gather the curtain along the rod into the final hanging folds while the glue is wet, or else it will be too stiff to move along. The rods themselves can be glued directly to the wall, or small wooden beads can be attached to the rod ends and the beads glued to the wall. The best method is to suspend the rod from two tiny eye-screws in the wall. Fancy glass beads on each end of the rod look attractive as well as preventing the rod from falling off the hooks.

Pelmets may be constructed over curtain-tops, and made either of balsa wood or cardboard.

Little roller blinds are quite effective if used on a window without curtains, such as in a bathroom. Simply roll a short length of fabric on to 3 mm dowel, let sufficient fabric hang to the length required permanently, and glue it into place. Add a tiny fringe and a blind pull. This can be made by hanging a single link from an old necklace clasp on a few strands of embroidery thread.

Manchester

When my two little grand-daughters visited me recently I did not have time before they arrived to fix the broken arm of my elderly miniature doll. Rather than have to admit that a doll was broken, I hastily put her in her dollhouse bed and told the children that granny was ill and could not see them today. As the children always bring some of their own doll family when they visit me, the sad message was instantly relayed to the doll visitors, who on this occasion happened to be two furry mice in velvet dresses. In hushed, squeaky voices and with much deliberation the children hurried out to my garden and picked some microscopic bunches of allysum which were then wrapped in wisps of tissue paper. The little visitors then quietly crept in to see poor sick granny, laying the flowers beside her, and in soft whispers told her all the news from home.

The scene was very touching. It could not have been achieved if granny had been lying rigidly on a bare wooden bed. Instead, her head was on a soft pillow, her shoulders were covered with sheets and blankets, her slippers were beside the bed, and a few things she needed were on a bedside table.

A miniature bed can indeed be soft and inviting if properly made up. The mattress should yield to the touch, and is ideally made of 12 mm plastic foam cut to the size of the bed and covered with striped or floral 'ticking'. Tufts can be made by stitching through the thickness with black cotton.

Sheets can be made of lawn or batiste, cut large enough to tuck under the mattress, and with a tiny hem all around. Hand-sewn hems are often clumsy on such a small scale, so machine-stitch if it is possible. This applies to all miniature manchester. The top sheet would look very distinctive if hand-embroidered with colours to match the room.

Blankets are made from fine warm material, plain or check-patterned. They look very real if bound all around with soft nylon ribbon, or if the edges are embroidered with blanket stitch. Otherwise it suffices to machine around the raw edges with zig-zag stitch to prevent fraying. One blanket is usually enough for each bed but a few extra could be made and kept in a wardrobe drawer for use on cold nights.

The 'piece de resistance' in bedrooms is always the bedspread. Here are a few ideas:
— Fitted satin with piped edges and pleats
— A throwover-style of silk brocade with a silk fringe
— A gaily patterned cotton patchwork throwover
— Checked gingham with smocking or cross-stitched embroidery
— A white lace spread with an underslip of coloured nylon

Any fabric at all can be prettily quilted, frilled, fringed or decorated with lace, braid or rosettes of ribbon.

Nursery beds look best with a throwover-style bedspread, plain or patterned, perhaps with a fringed edge or appliqued with a nursery motif. For bassinets small squares of crocheted or knitted wool with a minute bow or motif stitched on one corner are most appealing.

Sometimes the sides of bedspreads tend to stand out untidily from the bed, but this is remedied by putting a few stitches on the inside of each corner.

Continental quilts are fashionable today and provide another touch of comfort in the bedroom. They are made by stitching together two squares of suitable fabric, filling with a very small amount of cotton-wool and adding a few rows of machined quilting.

Pillows are made from plastic foam covered with the same material as the sheets or, if they are to be used as a decoration, they can be covered to match the bedspread. Tiny cushions for chairs are made the same way and are attractive if made of embroidered ribbon or all-over lace. Cushions for the kitchen should match the curtains and have little tapes to tie them to the back of the chair.

Do not forget towels for the bathroom. These can be cut from thin facecloths, plain or floral, edged with a single row of zig-zagging and with a narrow silk fringe stitched on each end. Silk (or synthetic) fringe is available at most haberdashery shops, but if it is a little too long for your needs, attach it first to the towel and then trim it to the required length.

Tea-towels for the kitchen look very real in a checked pattern, and potholders can be made of some bright material to catch the eye. Give potholders a tiny loop on one corner so that they may be hung near the stove.

Miniature doilies are necessary too, for dressing tables or side tables. If you can crochet, make them of the finest cotton, but if you cannot make them yourself, use a single medallion from a length of val lace.

You will need table mats for the dining room. These can be made on the same principle as the doilies, or they can be made of fabric with fringed edges. Tiny serviettes with fringed ends can be made to match, then rolled into serviette rings that are produced by cutting a strong plastic drinking straw into 3 mm lengths. Have you ever had a pretty but useless lace handkerchief given to you? If it is soft enough it would make an elegant dinner cloth to put in the sideboard drawer.

Accessories

All the Little Bits and Pieces

When the first tentative ideas of furnishing a miniature house begin to blossom, it is time to start collecting all the items that will make the house a home. Within a short time the search, which usually begins only half-seriously, becomes a happy obsession. Now you find yourself haunting junk jewellery counters, attending every fete with a white elephant stall, and looking thoughtfully at every single thing that once you would have thrown out automatically. You find yourself asking surprised friends for any odds and ends they might have finished with — or, you add without shame, any odds and ends they haven't finished with. You become a hoarder of beads, broken jewellery, buckles and buttons, lucky charms, party novelties, old compact mirrors, scraps of lace, ribbon, fabric, fur, vinyl, discarded artificial flowers, mail-order catalogues, bottle tops, toothpaste tube tops, lipstick cases, toothpicks, pieces of wire, cocktail sticks, in fact anything and everything. You know you have become addicted when you find yourself eagerly waiting for more junk advertising mail to be put in your letterbox, for it contains all kinds of paper goodies to add to your collection. I realised how seriously I had become involved when I bought a box of chocolates just to get the coloured wrapping foil! Before very long it is necessary to beg some empty shoeboxes from the local store to hold all the treasures — one for jewellery, one for coloured advertisements, one for fabric pieces, one for miscellany.

There eventually comes a time when the dollhouse is ready for its decorations and the assessment of wealth begins — wooden beads for making furniture; glass beads for light fittings and bottles; earrings for door knockers, light fittings, candlestick holders and letter racks; bottle tops for pie tins and plant-pots; advertisements for making clocks, books and groceries; charms for ornaments; buckles for picture frames; wire for coat-hangers; vinyl for bookcovers, and so on.

Accessories in the miniature house are the most challenging and rewarding part of the entire project. They include everything that a real house contains such as statues, vases of flowers, shopping baskets, jewellery, children's toys, perfume bottles, family photos, correspondence, books and magazines. Some of these things, reduced to diminutive proportions, become objects of fragile beauty and, as they are handmade, each could be regarded as a collector's item.

The only accessories that are really difficult to make are the cooking and eating utensils and

cutlery, and it is better to buy these items ready-made. Although tiny cups, saucers and plates are available in china, plastic is often preferable as there is a greater range of related tableware. Also, given an undercoat and final coat of paint, these lowly items assume the delicate appearance of porcelain. Colourful floral or border designs can be painted on them to produce exclusive miniature dinner sets. An extra touch of class can be given by adding a fine rim of gold around each edge — finicky perhaps, but well worth the effort.

Once a small girl, looking with wide eyes at the contents of a dollhouse, asked me if they were 'all really true things that got shrunk down'! That would certainly be a novel method of doing it, but not nearly so much fun!

Food

A kitchen without food is sad indeed, even in a dollhouse. It requires very little effort to provide a plate of cakes or a loaf of bread or a delectable fruit pie. Some foods can be purchased but they are generally mass-produced, expensive and not even very appealing. It is far better and much more satisfying to produce your own.

Pretend food can be made from dough in much the same way as we prepare real food, but with the addition of a very high percentage of salt to help in preservation. A mixture of crumbled bread and white glue will also produce pretend food. However, items containing real ingredients are likely to break if dropped, and if they are not cooked properly they will also go mouldy later. Also, in spite of the unpalatable additives, a wandering mouse might think it a veritable feast, and devour all your painstaking efforts — a compliment to the cook, no doubt, but one not likely to be appreciated!

A successful method of making food is to use modelling plastic. Although similar in appearance to plasticine, it becomes permanently hard after baking in an ordinary household oven. Recipes for a variety of foods will be found in the final chapter of this book. Once you begin to make pretend food you will find it hard to stop!

The Residents

In dollhouses there are good tenants and there are bad tenants, just as there are in real life. Bad tenants do nothing for the house. They merely sit around with stiff limbs and vacant faces. Some of them have never heard of the 1:12 scale and are foolishly too large or too small. On the other hand, good tenants enhance their surroundings by being sufficiently supple to sit in chairs with a certain amount of grace and their size complements the surroundings. The moral of this comparison is to demonstrate that even the most carefully furnished dollhouse can be spoilt by including unsuitable dolls. It is better to have no tenants at all than to have bad ones.

There are many miniature dolls on the market, and it pays to search around to find the right kind. You could even try making your own — at least they would have individuality. Have you ever noticed that nobody ever grows old in the doll world? This is fortunate for them, of course, but it would be nice to see a comfortable old person around the house now and then.

In earlier times home-made dolls were made of clothes pegs that were prettily painted and dressed. They can still be made, and wooden dolly pegs are available at most craft shops along with pipecleaners for making flexible arms. Peg dolls would be most suited to a tall Victorian villa with lots of frilly curtains and fussy furniture and where the residents would be expected to stand circumspectly in a corner or beside the fireplace.

For dolls to be capable of both standing and sitting, moving their arms and turning their heads, flexible limbs and bodies are essential. And for dolls that have dimension and expression in their faces, sculpturing is essential. With just a little effort we can put these two essentials together.

Making a Miniature Doll

The materials required are some pink or white pipecleaners 10 mm in diameter; a small amount of pale pink stretch fabric; some flesh-coloured modelling plastic (from a craft shop); and some fast-drying acetate glue (from a hobby shop). Tools for this work must be small — the implements found in a manicure set are quite good. If you are on very friendly terms with your dentist, ask him for any old instruments he can spare, as these are ideal.

The Head

Knead a marble-sized piece of modelling plastic and roll it into a ball 20 mm in diameter. Insert a very thin stick, such as 5 mm diameter dowel, halfway in to serve as a handle as you work and to provide the necessary recess in the neck for fitting the head to the body later. Model the face, not forgetting the ears, and form a neck approximately 6 mm long. Use a smear of water if you have difficulty in smoothing any area. The finished adult size should be about 20 mm from the top of the head to the chin (Fig. 16) and a child's size should be about 12 mm. If first attempts fail, simply roll up the plastic and start again. When satisfied with your work, allow about 48 hours to dry out, then harden it in the household oven according to the instructions on the packet. After the head has cooled, remove the piece of dowel.

The Body

Place two pipecleaners side by side. Measure 62 mm from the top end and secure together with a piece of cotton. Below the cotton separate the pipecleaners to form two legs (Fig. 17a). Measure down each leg about 80 mm, bend the leg back sharply and return to the top, winding surplus around the spine (Fig. 17b). Take a third pipecleaner and form a cross with the spine about 25 mm from the top, coiling around the spine once (Fig. 17c). Measure from the centre of the spine along each arm 60 mm, bend the arm sharply back, return it to the top and wind the surplus around the spine (Fig. 17d). The armature, or skeleton, is now completed and needs to be covered. Child-size dolls would be approximately three-quarters of the armature measurements depending on the age of the child required.

The Covering

Cut four strips from the fabric, each 30 mm wide and 12 mm longer than the limb being covered, having the stretch of the fabric across the width. Fold each strip in halves lengthwise and, using a small stitch, machine along the raw edge and curve around one end, 5 mm in from the edge (Fig. 18a). Trim the seam to 3 mm and carefully turn the tube right side out. Push the arms and legs into their respective casings, using a movement as though putting on gloves. Pull them high on each limb to a firm fit and stitch down (Fig. 18b). If you are making a matronly doll, glue a little cotton-wool on to supply a bust — but don't overdo it! Now cut some fabric into strips 12 mm wide and wind it firmly around the body, using a spot of glue here and there to keep it in place and taking care to have a neat finish around the neck (Fig. 18c). Bend each foot to the front about 20 mm. The wrists may be suggested by tightly winding a thread of pink cotton around the wrist area and adding a spot of glue.

Later on, when you wish to experiment, you could try making the hands and shoe-encased feet out of modelling plastic, using the same method of construction as was used in the making of the head. Each hand would include the forearm to the elbow, and the foot would include the leg to just under the knee. This system supplies very dainty hands and feet and solves the problem of making shoes.

Attaching the Head

The plastic neck should fit down neatly to the top of the arms. If the spine is too long, bend it over — it should be a tight fit inside the neck recess. However, if the spine does not fit in, simply snip off the 'wool' from the pipecleaners. Pour a little glue into the neck recess and add more glue to the top of the spine before inserting it. If there is any space to spare in the recess, press in some cotton-wool and more glue. Allow it to dry adequately, preferably overnight. Paint the face by merely touching the pupils of the eyes with blue or brown paint and the lips with a little red. Put some red on your finger and rub it softly on the cheeks, fading out the edges for natural colouring. Do not over-paint or the effect will be clown-like.

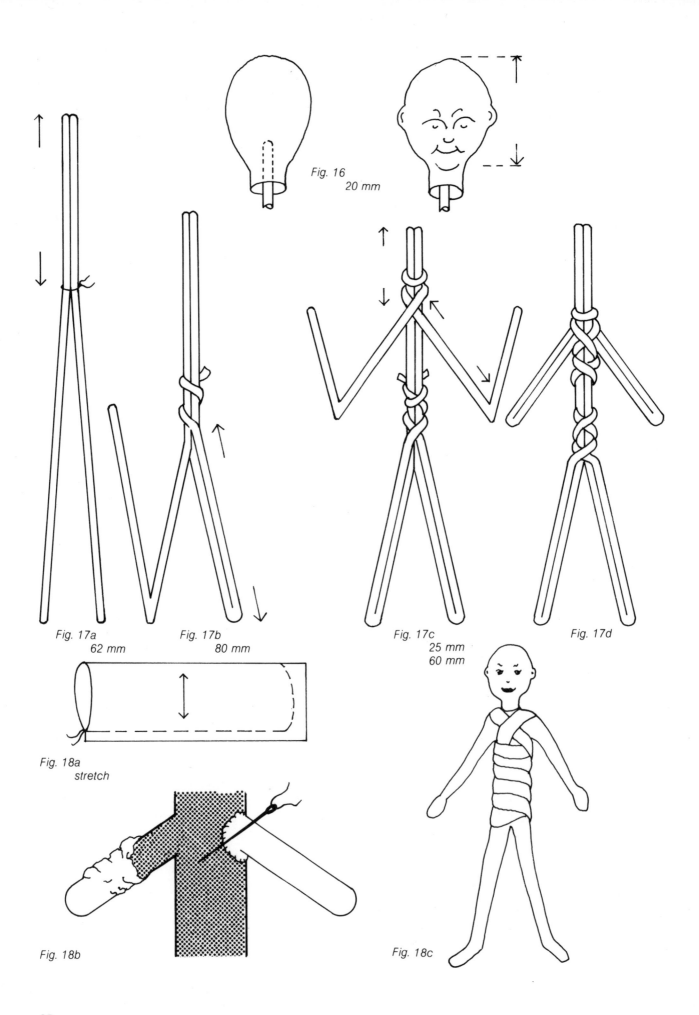

Fig. 16
20 mm

Fig. 17a
62 mm

Fig. 17b
80 mm

Fig. 17c
25 mm
60 mm

Fig. 17d

Fig. 18a
stretch

Fig. 18b

Fig. 18c

The Hair

Select the most natural colour of knitting wool to suit the doll. Cut the strands longer than you think you will need — the correct length can be cut later when the work is done. A number of different styles can be made from the following simple method.

Measure the distance between the top of the forehead and the base of the skull (Fig. 19). Cut lengths of the wool and closely bunch them together on a piece of tissue paper until they equal this measurement across. Using a small stitch, machine through the centre with a backstitch at the start and finish (Fig. 20). This stitching forms the centre parting. Remove the paper. Unravel each strand of wool then gently brush it, taking care not to pull the stitches. The hair is now ready to be glued on to the head.

Straight hair: Arrange the hair nicely around the forehead and smooth it evenly around the head. Cut to the required length, usually just below the ears (Fig. 21).

Plaited hair: Draw the hair over the ears and plait it to the length needed. Cut off the surplus and tie the ends of the plaits with narrow ribbon or embroidery cotton (Fig. 22).

Bunched hair: Draw the hair to each side and fasten it with ribbons. Allow the hair to reach the shoulders and trim off any surplus (Fig. 23).

Back bun: Pull the hair carefully down over the ears and turn up towards the back of the head. Twist or coil it into a bun and glue it well, tucking in all stray ends. Glue the hair to the ears (Fig. 24).

Fringe: To add a fringe, simply pull a few of the front strands over the forehead and cut off neatly to the length required. Do not let any glue get on the fringe, but have it hanging loose (Fig. 23). The fringe may be applied to any style.

Hair for a male doll: Take a length of wool and chop it finely into fluff with scissors. Put some glue on the head just where the hair is required. Holding the doll by the body dip the head into the fluff until all the glue is covered, then pat it down. If the gentleman is to have a partly bald head or a receding hairline, do not put glue in those areas (Fig. 25). A moustache or beard, if needed, is made the same way.

This method can also be used for short-haired females, but in this case allow the hair to 'grow' over the ears and lower down the back of the neck to appear more feminine.

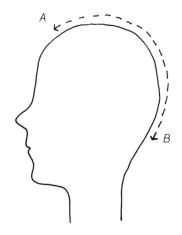

Fig. 19
Head measurement

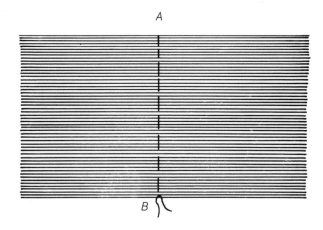

Fig. 20
Making the hair

Fig. 21
Straight hair

Fig. 22
Plaited hair

Fig. 23
Bunched hair

Fig. 24
Back bun

Fig. 25
Hair styles for male dolls

The interior of Blossom Cottage.

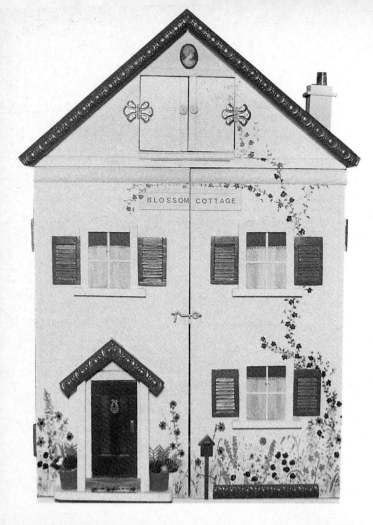

The exterior of Blossom Cottage. The tiny doors at the top when open allow a peek into an attic filled with antique treasures.

Mr Blossom relaxes by a glowing fire.

Mrs Blossom in her kitchen. She is busily knitting while Fido snoozes in his basket on the hearth.

The master bedroom at Linley Court. The door shown partly open is a walk-in wardrobe which conveniently fits beneath a hall stairway leading to the attic above. The bed is comfortably made up with mattress, sheets and blankets beneath the lace bedspread. Miniature roses are in the vase on the dressing-table and on the shelf under the bedside table are several novels suitable for late night reading.

The exterior of Linley Court. The roof lifts up to expose the children's playroom and nursery bedroom which take up the entire floor. The front doors of the house are hinged in the centre to fold back upon themselves to save space. Painted flowers growing in the front garden continue around the sides of the house.

The kitchen at Linley Court is a bright and cheerful room. The refrigerator (made from balsa wood) is well stocked with bottles of milk (made of chalk) and frozen chickens (made of modelling plastic wrapped in supermarket advertisements). Some of the recipe books have recipes printed inside. The fruit in the bowl is made from modelling plastic, the condiment jars are made from wooden beads, and the clock is a picture of a clock glued on wood cut to shape.

In a corner of the lounge room at Linley Court is an upright piano complete with music. The piano is made from balsa wood and is handsomely decorated with 'carving' achieved by using glued-on lace. Fancy supporting parts are formed by wooden beads. The keys are from a piano advertisement. The stool is of balsa wood with legs made by wooden beads threaded onto toothpicks. On the wall above is a frame carved from balsa wood and its picture is a European postage stamp.

A wider view of the lounge room reveals that coffee and cakes are on the table waiting for visitors. The lampshade of the standard lamp is made of cream lace over red silk, and the cushions are decorative ribbon filled with cotton wool. The leopard skin mat has a stuffed head with brown bead eyes and a red felt tongue and is the room's conversation piece. Postage stamp pictures on the walls are framed with carved balsa wood and the portrait on the bookcase is framed by a metal brooch. The busts on the mantlepiece are made from plastic toy figures cut down, mounted on wooden bases, and then painted.

The interior of Rainbow Arcade shopping centre. On the inside of the enclosing doors (which are not displayed in the picture) are painted wrought iron stairways that lead from the ground floor where we find the greengrocer, grocer, ice-cream shop and butcher, to the next floor and the toy shop, boutique and doctor's surgery, and on to the top level to the dressmaker's shop and the cafe.

Joe's fruit and vegetable shop in Rainbow Arcade. Joe the greengrocer is cutting up some pumpkin. His stock is made from modelling plastic — apples, pears, oranges, bananas, lettuce, potatoes, carrots, strawberries and grapes. The pineapples, however, are tiny cones from real trees and have been painted yellow.

Opposite page

Top: *Arcadia Cafe. The lady is waiting for the customer to make a choice. Supplies of crockery and cutlery and trays are on the bottom shelf. The door in the right wall leads to where the chef slaves away in his kitchen.*

Bottom left: *Mrs Cotton's shop in Rainbow Arcade. Mrs Cotton the dressmaker is cutting out a dress. The pattern (made from real pattern paper) is set out on the fabric, and the scissors (cut out from thin aluminium) are ready at hand. Her tape measure is made from narrow ribbon and marked with a pen. The wool is real and is wrapped in bands cut from wool advertisements.*

Bottom right: *The doctor's surgery at Rainbow Arcade. The doctor is ready for any emergencies. Around his neck is his stethoscope which is made from wire and dress eyelets. Bottles of medicine are tiny perfume sample bottles with bead stoppers. The sink and examination couch are of balsa wood, and wall pictures are cut out from medical advertisements and mounted on board.*

Jam Tarts 20c   Iced Cakes 40c   Donuts 20c   Strawberry Pie 95c   Extra Cream 20c   Ice Cream 70c   Choc Pudding 90c

Sandwiches $1.25   Meat Pie & Vegs. $2.50   Fish & Chips $2.75   Chop & Veges $3.50   Sausages & Eggs $3.00

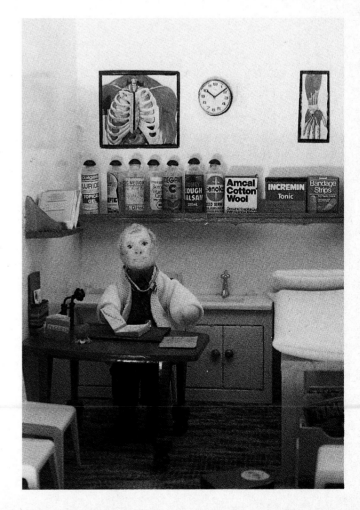

Mr Coffee's grocery shop in Rainbow Arcade. All the items are hand-made excepting the miniature cash register. The cakes and breads are made from modelling plastic or treated dough. Most of the other articles are tiny shapes of wood covered with suitable advertisements. One cheese has been nibbled by a mouse and if you look you will find him on the shelf in the top left-hand corner.

The schoolhouse. The door opens down to provide a lawn (of artificial grass from a hobby shop) and flowers in planter boxes. The teacher lives upstairs and her room is well furnished for eating and sleeping. Downstairs is the schoolroom with seating for eight children. All of the toys are educational and there are books on most subjects as well as a class scrapbook. There are plenty of children's music books on the piano. Perhaps the child who drew the picture of teacher on the blackboard has made amends by putting the apple on her desk!

Clothing for Miniature Dolls

Miniature dolls require tiny and intricate clothes. Removable garments are neither easy nor practical so it is far better to glue them on. To satisfy a child, perhaps, a few removable items such as coats, aprons and hats could be supplied.

It is important to attach the clothes in the correct order — females have panties first, then petticoat, then frock. Males have shirt first, then trousers, then coat. Failure to observe this rule could have some disastrous results, such as Father Doll having his trousers glued on first and forever being unable to tuck in his shirt.

Use non-fraying materials whenever possible because hems and edges on such small garments are difficult to sew neatly, and hems can be dispensed with if the fabric does not fray. Use small-patterned fabrics to suit the size of the dolls. Buttons are usually tiny glass beads, but while working on the miniature clothes they will be referred to as buttons.

White glue is normally safe to use on clothing but if you have any doubts, purchase some fabric glue from a craft shop. Whatever glue you use, use it very sparingly: one small dot here and there is usually sufficient.

The sizes and patterns provided below are for the average-sized miniature hand-made doll and may require slight modification according to the doll you are dressing. As all hand-made dolls vary slightly in size — no matter how much we try to keep them uniform — you may find that the given patterns are too large, or too small, or too short, or too long. Fortunately they are easy to adjust. If you make any little garments that for some reason do not fit the doll, do not throw them away. Make some tiny coat-hangers from balsa wood and hang the clothes in one of the wardrobes.

Just for the enjoyment of making them, why not add an evening dress or two, a tennis dress, or a dressing gown? Put some baby gowns and jackets in the nursery drawer. There is no limit to what you can produce, and eventually you will have the best-dressed doll family in town!

Clothes for Female Dolls

Panties

Make brief panties for the younger females and bloomers to the knee for the older generation. If the skirt is to be a tight-fitting style, panties may not be needed at all, or just stitch a row of narrow lace across the tops of the legs and catch together with a stitch underneath. On miniature dolls the shape of the panties is not crucial.

To make a simple pair of panties, cut a piece of material 70 mm × 30 mm. Sew narrow lace on one long edge. Join the two short edges to form a back seam. Turn the garment right side out and put it on the doll. Catch together at the crotch with a stitch. Trim the top to meet the waist level, put a row of stitching around the waistline and gather in tightly (Fig. 26).

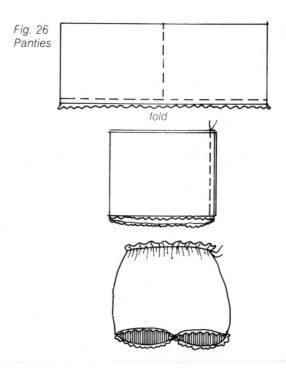

*Fig. 26
Panties*

fold

Bloomers

Trace the pattern provided. Cut two pieces of fabric. Machine the centre front edges together, then the centre back edges together. With the centre front seam facing the front, stitch around the inside legs and crotch. Trim and clip the curves, and turn the garment right side out. Put it on the doll and if the waist is too high trim off the excess. Gather around the top edge and pull in tightly. Tuck under raw edges of the legs at knee level, stitch on narrow lace and gather it tightly (Fig. 27).

Petticoats

These are necessary from the waist down only. Take a piece of broderie anglaise about 70 mm wide and cut it twice the hip measurement. Fold it over and stitch the short edge to form a back seam. Turn the garment right side out. Measure the length required and cut off any excess from the top edge. Put the petticoat on the doll, gather around the top and pull it in tightly, stitching securely (Fig. 28). If preferred any fine fabric may be used, with or without trimming.

Fig. 27
Bloomers

Dresses and Blouses

Hand-made dolls usually look more attractive with high necklines that can be prettily finished with collars or ruffles. Long sleeves are preferable also, but this depends on how well the doll's arms have been made. Tiny dresses are easier to make if they are sewn separately in three parts — the sleeves, the bodice and the skirt — and attached to the doll in that order. The instructions given here apply to the making of dresses. However, if the bodice and skirt are made of different materials or colours they become to all appearances a blouse and skirt.

Sleeves: Cut a piece of fabric 50 mm × 45 mm. Turn over the raw edge on one short end and machine it down to make a tiny hem. Fold the sleeve lengthwise, right sides together, and stitch the seam. Turn the sleeve right side out. Slide it on to the arm of the doll, check the length and allow for any cuff to be added. Cut off excess at the shoulder end, but it is important to allow enough material to stitch across the body of the doll (Fig. 29a). Make the second sleeve the same way.

Fig. 28
Petticoat

Lace cuff: Stitch some narrow lace around the end of the sleeve while turning the hem.

Frilled cuff: After the sleeve has been put on the doll, cut some narrow lace to measure twice the circumference of the wrist and gather it tightly into place (Fig. 29b).

Banded cuff: Gather the end of the sleeve into the wrist. Cut a narrow piece of fabric (or selvedge) and fold it so that the raw edges are underneath. After the sleeve has been put on the doll, glue the cuff firmly into place, covering the end of the sleeve. Stitch on a button (Fig. 29c).

Short sleeves: Make in the same way as the long sleeves but at the desired length. Cuffs may be added in the same way.

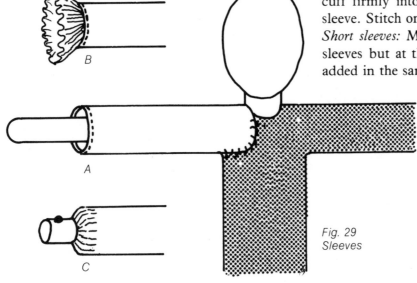

Fig. 29
Sleeves

Crossover bodice: Cut two strips of fabric each 25 mm × 100 mm. Turn all four long edges under narrowly, and stitch down. Fit one piece diagonally across the torso of the doll, keeping high around the neck, and stitch together where the sides meet at the underarm. Fit the other piece on the doll in the same manner, thus forming a crossover bodice back and front. Trim the ends to extend no more than 12 mm below the waistline. Add a collar if you wish, or catch the front edge together with a tiny flower or a bead to represent a brooch (Fig. 30).

Fig. 30
Crossover bodice

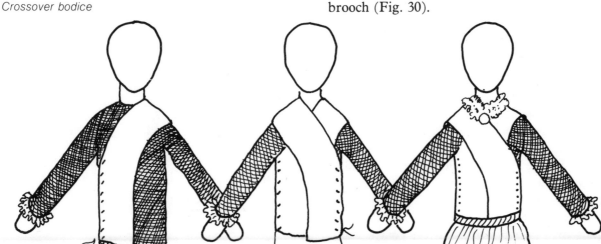

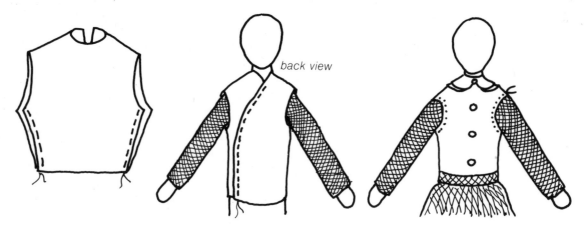

Plain bodice: Trace the pattern provided and cut out one piece of fabric. Put the underarms together and stitch. Turn the garment right side out and put it on the doll. Fold the back of the bodice one side over the other, adjusting to the size of the body. If the doll has very sloped shoulders, remove the bodice and (on the wrong side) machine a shoulder seam to take in the excess. Replace the bodice on the doll. Keep the neckline high at the front. Adjust the back, cut off any excess, and when you are satisfied with the fit turn under the raw edge at the back and stitch down neatly. This fold-over at the back can be left on the diagonal or cut off to form a straight back seam. With a needle turn under the raw edges around the armholes and stitch the armholes to the sleeves. Make a collar or frill for the neck (Fig. 31).

Bodice with magyar sleeves: As this style has the sleeves incorporated in the pattern, separate sleeves will not have to be made. The style may be used with the centre seam either at the front or the back, and it is particularly suited to fine stretch fabrics. Trace the pattern provided. Cut out one piece of material. Mark in the centre line. Hold the cut-out fabric against the doll to determine the length of sleeve required. Cut off the surplus and turn under the raw edge to a narrow hem. Fold the garment where indicated on the shoulder line and sew along each sleeve/underarm, 6 mm in from the edge. Trim and clip the curves. Cut open the centre line to the neck, then cut open the slight neck allowance cautiously — you can continue to enlarge it if needed, depending on the size of the doll. Fit the garment on the doll and if necessary take in a little more of the sleeve/underarm seams. Turn the bodice right side out. Put it on the doll, turn under one side of the centre seam, fold it over the raw edge of the other side and stitch it down to close the opening. Add cuffs and neck trimmings. Buttons may be stitched along the centre seam (Fig. 32).

Fig. 31
Plain bodice

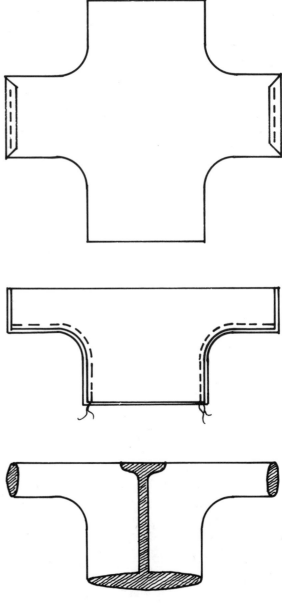

Fig. 32
Bodice with magyar sleeves

Example of magyar bodice

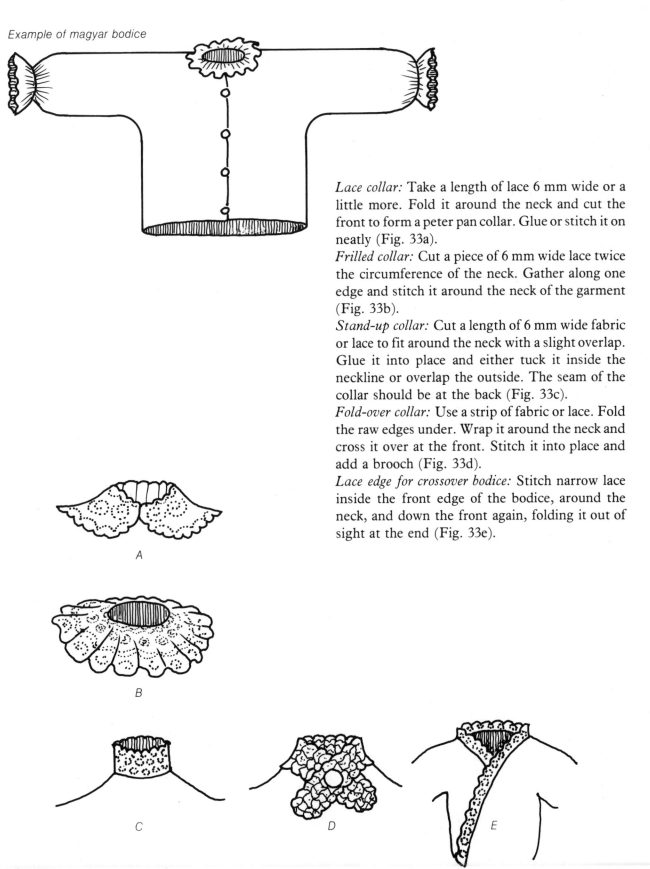

Lace collar: Take a length of lace 6 mm wide or a little more. Fold it around the neck and cut the front to form a peter pan collar. Glue or stitch it on neatly (Fig. 33a).

Frilled collar: Cut a piece of 6 mm wide lace twice the circumference of the neck. Gather along one edge and stitch it around the neck of the garment (Fig. 33b).

Stand-up collar: Cut a length of 6 mm wide fabric or lace to fit around the neck with a slight overlap. Glue it into place and either tuck it inside the neckline or overlap the outside. The seam of the collar should be at the back (Fig. 33c).

Fold-over collar: Use a strip of fabric or lace. Fold the raw edges under. Wrap it around the neck and cross it over at the front. Stitch it into place and add a brooch (Fig. 33d).

Lace edge for crossover bodice: Stitch narrow lace inside the front edge of the bodice, around the neck, and down the front again, folding it out of sight at the end (Fig. 33e).

A

B

C

D

E

Fig. 33
Necklines

Skirts

The length of the skirt is the measurement from the waist down to the required length, allowing a little extra for a hem (if a hem is necessary). The width is twice the measurement around the hips, or just a little more if the fabric is particularly fine. Cut out the material in one piece. Fold it in halves and stitch it to form a back seam. Stitch the hem. Turn the skirt right side out and put it on the doll. Gather the top edge, pull it in very firmly, and stitch it to the bodice. Add a narrow waistband to cover the join (Fig. 34).

Variations for the skirt:
— Add a frill of the same fabric or lace to the hem
— Add a flower or trailing ribbon to the waist
— Add a row of buttons or braid down the centre front
— Add ornamental pockets
— Add rows of lace or braid around the skirt horizontally (Fig. 35).

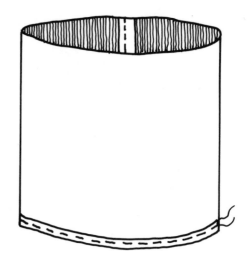

Fig. 34
Skirt

Fig. 35
Variations for the skirt

30

One-piece Frock

This style is quick and easy to make. Simply make the bodice with magyar sleeves as instructed, but when cutting out the pattern extend the waistline down to the length of dress required. Turn under the raw edge at the hemline if necessary. The opening of this dress may be at the back or the front. Finish it with any of the variations suggested for the neckline and sleeves. A ruffle running down the full length of the front looks attractive. Add a narrow belt or sash, unless the dress is for an 'elderly' doll, in which case the waist is better left undefined (Fig. 36).

Coat

Use a soft, non-fraying material. Make up the bodice with magyar sleeves as instructed, but when cutting out the pattern extend the waistline to the length of coat required (hip or knee length). Have the opening to the front. Ensure that there is ample room for the coat to fit the fully dressed doll with ease. Carefully cut out the neckline, curving it gently on the front corners. Add patch or flap pockets. Stitch some buttons down the left front edge (Fig. 37).

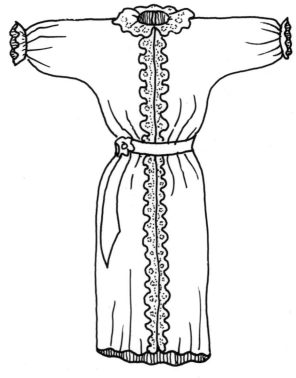

Fig. 36
One-piece frock

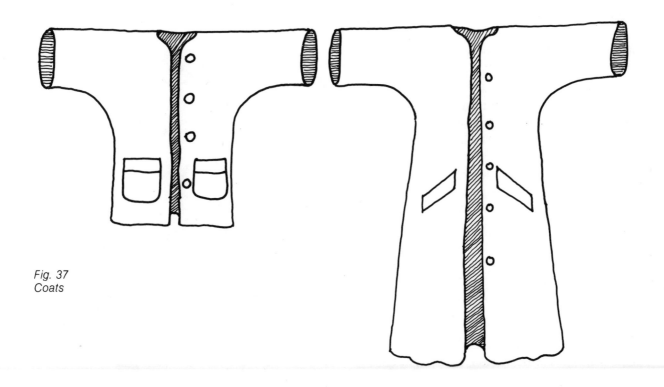

Fig. 37
Coats

Clothes for Little Girl Dolls

Follow the same instructions as given for the female dolls, but trace the pattern on the inside dotted lines. Make the sleeves in the same way as suggested, but cut the fabric to 40 mm × 45 mm. As children vary in size, seams will need to be adjusted as you proceed. When attaching the skirt, raise the waistline to just under the arms to give the dress a more youthful appearance.

Variations for the dresses:
— Add lace or frills to the hem to match collar and cuffs
— Thread ribbon through eyelet lace at the waistline
— Stitch rows of lace around the skirt horizontally
— Stitch on a frilly pinafore
— Attach a sash with a bow at the back
— Glue on pockets or appliques (Fig. 38).

Clothes for Male Dolls

Coats and trousers can be made from thin felt or any soft material that does not fray easily. Shirts can be of lightweight stretch material. If a coat is to be worn, shirts need not be whole garments, but the front portion only will suffice, as the coat will hide the back and sleeve areas providing it is discreetly glued or stitched in the right places.

To make a tie, knot one end of a piece of narrow ribbon and glue the knot close to the shirt collar.

Fig. 38
Dresses for little girl dolls

Shirt

Follow the instructions for making the bodice with magyar sleeves. Have the opening at the front and adjust the length so that the shirt will tuck neatly into the top of the trousers. Cut off any excess. Make a banded cuff on the sleeves. A pocket is optional. Make the collar from a length of the fabric (a selvedge is helpful) 12 mm wide and long enough to go around the neck. Mark where both ends meet at the centre front and cut off slantwise to form collar peaks. Stand the collar up on the inside of the neck edge and stitch together lightly (or carefully glue them). Turn the collar down to the outside. Sew buttons on the front seamline (Fig. 39).

Coat

Follow the instructions for making the coat for female dolls but add the buttons to the right side of the front opening.

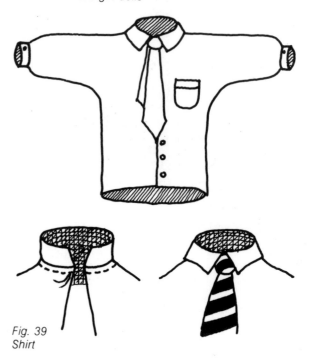

Fig. 39
Shirt

Trousers

Trace the pattern provided and cut out two pieces of fabric. With the right sides facing, machine the centre front seams together and the centre back seams together. Try the garment against the doll to establish the length of legs, cut off any surplus and turn under the raw edges if necessary. Open the trousers so that the centre front seam faces the front and stitch around the inside legs and crotch. Try the trousers on the doll and if the legs are too wide stitch the seam again to reduce them. Trim and clip the curve and turn the garment right side out. Put the trousers on the doll and trim the top down to waist level. Tuck in the shirt and put a few stitches around the waist to secure the clothes to the body. Add a narrow belt of the same material and glue it down (Fig. 40).

Variations for trousers:
— Make shorts by cutting the legs to knee level
— Make overalls by adding a square bib front, shoulder straps and patch pockets.

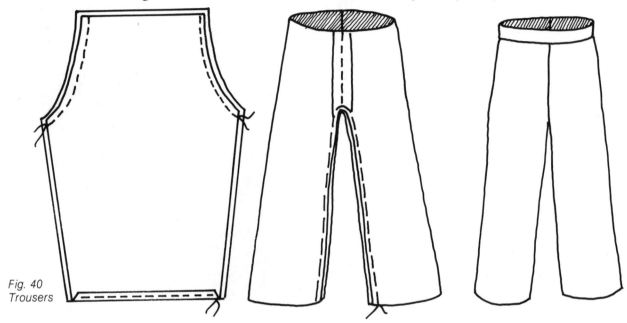

Fig. 40
Trousers

Clothes for Little Boy Dolls

Follow the same instructions as given for the male dolls but trace the patterns on the inside dotted lines. As children vary in size, the seams will need to be adjusted as you proceed.

Variations:
— Plain short trousers and a bright striped shirt
— Overalls with a crew-neck shirt or knitted jumper
— Short trousers with matching jacket and a bow tie (Fig. 41).

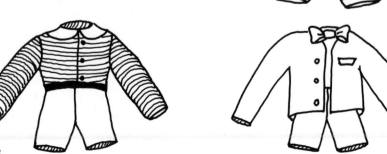

Fig. 41
Clothes for little boy dolls

Socks

Choose a thin stretch fabric, plain or striped. Cut two pieces, each about 30 mm wide by whatever length socks you require plus the length of the foot.

Socks can be ankle, calf or knee length, or they can become stockings by extending to the top of the leg.

Have the stretch of the fabric across the width. Fold each strip in halves lengthwise and machine along the raw edge with a narrow seam, curving around at one end. Trim the seam and turn the tube right side out (Fig. 42).

Shoes

Shoes and boots made of plastic can sometimes be purchased in packets of doll accessories from toy-shops. They can be improved by painting them and adding a rhinestone or bead to the front.

Otherwise shoes can be made from black felt. Trace the pattern provided and cut out the felt. Lay the upper on top of the sole, matching points A. Using tiny topstitching, join the upper to the sole, matching points B. Stitch up the back seam. If the shoe is too large, cut off the surplus length at point B. Glue the shoe on to the doll. For a female doll, cut the upper to the dotted line of the instep, and when the shoe is on the doll add a tiny felt strap and a button (Fig. 43).

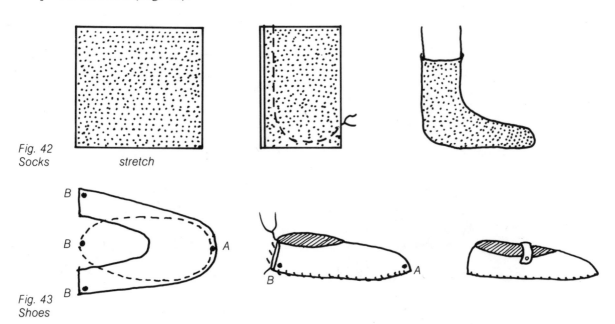

Fig. 42
Socks   stretch

Fig. 43
Shoes

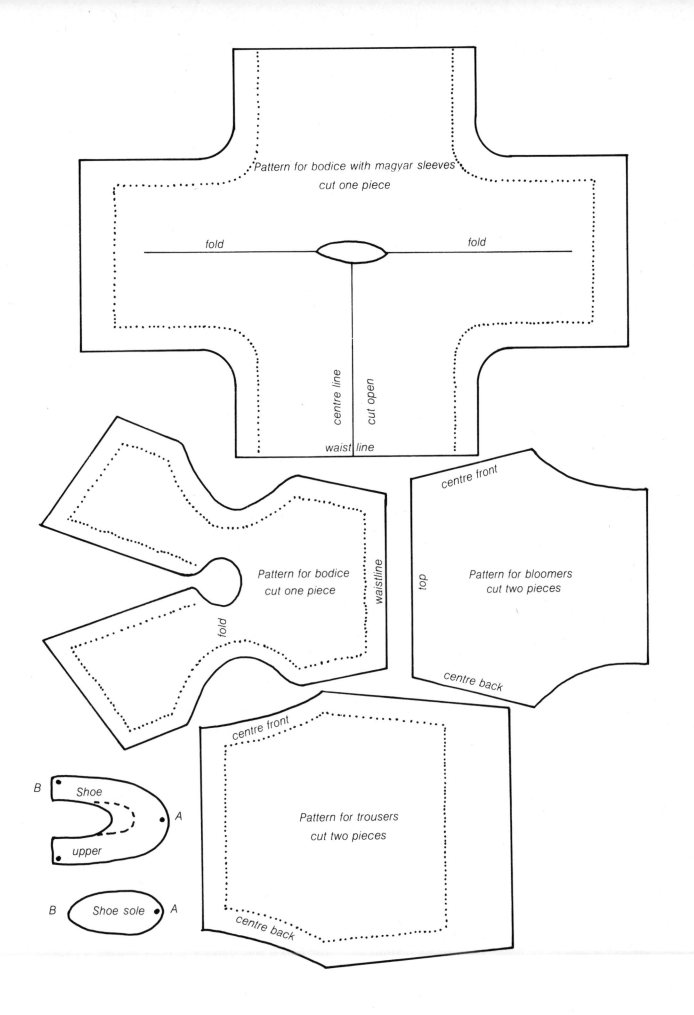

Pattern for bodice with magyar sleeves
cut one piece

fold   fold

centre line   cut open

waist line

Pattern for bodice
cut one piece

waistline

fold

centre front

top

Pattern for bloomers
cut two pieces

centre back

B   Shoe

A

upper

B   Shoe sole   A

centre front

Pattern for trousers
cut two pieces

centre back

Visiting the Miniature World

During the Great Depression few children had more than one or two toys and very few had dollhouses, for such things were luxuries. I had a little friend who shared some of my early childhood during that time and together we made our own dollhouse. It had no walls or roof but was composed of small sticks laid flat to form a ground plan with spaces for doorways. We planted real moss for a front lawn and the furniture was made of matchboxes. The dolls, which I still remember with affection, were pictures of dress models cut from newspaper advertisements. In spite of the fact that they usually had the price of the frock printed across their chest, we laboriously cut them out and suitably named each one before settling them into their new home. Although today's children live in a wonderland of toys, playing house in miniature is still one of their greatest joys.

Would you care to see some of the more recent dollhouses I have made? Would you like to knock on a tiny front door and be invited inside? Let us close our eyes for a moment and pretend to assume Lilliputian dimensions so that we will be able to wander through the rooms and see how they are furnished, and perhaps meet some of the little people who live there. Later, when the visiting is over and we have come back to being ourselves again, I will explain how many of the dollhouse accessories were made. Shall we go?

Linley Court

Linley Court is a family home that is painted cream with a green roof and green trimmings. The painted-on windows have lace curtains, fringed blinds and brown shutters, and there are also three dormer windows up in the roof. It is a dignified house with formal urns of roses painted on each side of the entrance, although other colourful flowers tumble in confusion along the walls.

Once inside the house we are faced with an elegant stairway that turns with a landing out of sight upstairs and is carpeted with red feltex. The newel posts are white-painted carved cedar and the balustrading, which at first glance appears to be wrought iron, is in fact clear solid plastic painted with a black wrought iron design. In the entrance hall is a small table with a telephone, a directory and a vase of flowers. Would you care to leave your hat on one of the hat hooks on the wall? The red and gold wallpaper is pretty, isn't it? The floor covering here is beige nylon carpet that runs through into the dining and lounge rooms.

The dining room is furnished with a teak-coloured table, matching carved sideboard and four chairs that are upholstered in green velvet. The wallpaper is self-patterned gold foil and is hung with prints of birds and with a large snow scene in a burnished frame. On the ceiling is an ornamental lightshade of blue crystal and gold. A tall candle in a gold filigree holder stands on the sideboard, flanked on one side by a silver beer stein and on the other by a gold-framed photograph of an elderly woman. The table is set with lace tablemats, cutlery for three courses, silver cruet set, cheese dish and cream jug, wine glasses and hand-painted plates. I wonder what the meal is going to be? Let's look in the kitchen.

A casserole is cooking in the oven and a kettle and a frying pan are on the stove top. It is a very modern kitchen with a brown vinyl floor and white and green built-in cupboards that match the gingham curtains. Under the window is the sink. The refrigerator is well stocked and has bottles of milk in the door racks. If we peep into the cupboard drawers we will find a supply of cutlery, some tea-towels and an apron for mother. Along the bench top stand a pop-up toaster, a dish of fruit, wooden cannisters of tea, coffee and sugar, bottles of sauce and wine, and a food blender. And there is a high chair in the corner for baby. On the yellow-papered walls hang cooking spoons, a wooden shelf with interesting recipe books, a pendulum clock and a calendar.

The lounge room is a very cosy place with red velvet and cream lace curtains and red velvet lounge chairs. A standard lamp with a silk and lace shade stands nearby, while overhead is a pearl chandelier. The wallpaper of silver and white stripes is a good background for the impressive wall pictures — a gold oval-framed portrait of a woman and child, a portrait of an elderly man, two English country scenes in carved frames, a modern painting of some children and, over the fireplace in a carved frame, a print of 'The Night-watch' by Rembrandt. The fireplace is of polished timber, and red embers are glowing warmly among the smouldering logs of wood. A fresh supply of firewood stands on the hearth next to the brass fireguard. On the mantelpiece are two white busts, a Victorian clock under glass and a few books. There are quite a lot of books in the book-case, covering such subjects as antiques, poetry, gardening and art, and on top of the bookcase are a picture of a baby in a silver frame and a silver letter holder containing several stamped, addressed letters.

Wouldn't it be nice if we could sit here at the fireside for a little while? The floral scatter cushions make the chairs very comfortable and there is a small tapestry-covered footstool for extra comfort. Perhaps someone could play the music that is set up on the ornate piano over there in the corner — there is an upholstered music stool to sit on. Do you like the vase of flowers on top of the piano? There are some magazines lying near a chair, along with a box of Cadbury's chocolates — and see, there are chocolates inside! The little round occasional table standing on the leopard-skin rug is set with cups and saucers, a silver coffee service, and a silver plate of tempting iced cakes. Perhaps visitors are expected, so we had better go upstairs out of the way.

On the stair landing we must pause a moment to look at the statue of a Spanish dancer, and to read the words 'Bless our Home' that are painted on the tall stained-glass window picturing an angel hovering over a cluster of little children. The lightshade above the deep stairwell is a lantern-style set with coloured glass.

The first room upstairs is the bathroom with pink and green floral walls, white marbled vinyl floor and a pink window-blind with lace scallop trimming. There is also a towel rail with a pink fringed towel, a set of weighing scales and a bathmat. The handbasin, bath and toilet are pink, and the light fitting is a sphere of white china. A cake of soap is on the handbasin.

Blue sets the theme for the guest room in the floral wallpaper, plush scatter rug and brocade slipper chair. The curtains are white scalloped lace. There is a silver-framed print of Tom Roberts' 'The Reconciliation' on the wall, and a pretty enamel and gold crucifix hangs over the white antique bed. The bedspread is white lace over blue silk and has a pillow to match. While nobody is looking we could turn the bedspread down and see a blue wool blanket, white vyella sheets and a blue striped mattress. A large mirror decorates the antique dressing table and reflects a gold bedroom clock and two perfume bottles standing on a lace doily. In the drawers are tissues, some Yardley's April Violets soap and talc, and a gold bracelet that a guest has left behind. Overhead is a glass-studded silver lightshade.

At the other end of the hall is the parents' bedroom with pink floral wallpaper, white lace curtains and a white furry scatter rug. A white frosted china ceiling light matches a reading lamp that stands on the bedside table alongside several popular novels. The modern bed is white-painted timber and is made up like the guest room bed, but with pink as the choice of colour, topped with a pink floral lace bedspread that has drawn-thread work on the frill. Identical lace forms a skirt around the kidney-shaped dressing table that is rather crowded with a gold clock, two perfume bottles, hand-mirror and comb, and a red rose in a metal vase. The little stool accompanying the dressing table has a mother-of-pearl seat. On the walls are a small mirror, a gold-framed picture of a mother and child, a religious picture and a set of diminutive silver-framed pictures of family members. The built-in wardrobe has plenty of space and fits neatly out of sight beneath a hall stairway leading to the attic.

We must hold on to the wooden handrail while treading our way up these steep narrow stairs. At the top we find ourselves in a very large children's playroom. Fawn feltex covers the floor of the attic, and there is a beige rug at one end on which stands four little red chairs and a red table with a game of draughts and a picture book on the top. Toys are scattered around — a rocker painted with horses, a pink pram with a doll in it, a wooden train, a pull-along car, a set of quoits and several other items. A bookshelf contains a television set and lots of books for children. There is also a cupboard with an ironing board and iron, a shopping basket, a feather duster and a broom. Next to this is the linen press stocked with extra towels, sheets, warm blankets and a couple of tartan bush rugs to take on picnics. The lightshades are multi-coloured balloon type and the wallpaper, which also decorates the nursery in the next room, is a busy design of fairies, flowers and kittens.

We should tiptoe into the nursery because baby is asleep, tucked under a pink cover in a lace-canopied bassinet. Alongside is a toddler's cot covered with a blue crocheted rug. Further along is a bed for a larger child with all the usual bedclothes under a patchwork throwover. There is a patterned brown scatter rug next to a chest of drawers that is loaded with bottles of Johnson's Baby Shampoo and Baby Lotion, a pile of folded napkins, spare safety pins and a baby's feeding bottle.

As we should not overstay our welcome, perhaps we will quietly leave the house now. Don't forget to pick up your hat on the way out. Just along the street is where Grannie and Grandad Blossom live, and I'm sure they would be pleased to see us.

Blossom Cottage

Blossom Cottage is a small old-fashioned place, suited to the two elderly folk living here. The walls are white and the roof and trimmings are chocolate brown, with the exception of the front door and the chimney top, which are bright red. Right up under the roof is an attic window. Isn't that a lovely red flowering plant climbing all over the front wall? The little garden is bright and pretty, too. There are flowers in the ornamental pots near the door and a cheerful red letterbox. A small porch roof is over the front door, which has a gold knocker and polished brass door plate, and on the much-worn doorstep is a 'welcome' mat.

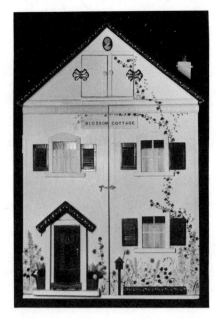

Inside we can see that the ground floor is all one room. The kitchen and sitting room are combined in a simple and country-like way, with a brown linoleum floor. Grannie is sitting down doing her knitting. She is dressed in a brown print dress with lace collar and cuffs and a white apron, and her broderie anglaise petticoat is hanging a little from under the long skirt. She beams at us with bright blue eyes. Grandad is in his cane-backed rocking chair reading the paper. He is a cheerful old fellow with a balding head and a gold watch on a chain across his waistcoat.

The table has not been cleared since their meal and is cluttered with a loaf of bread partly sliced by a red-handled bread knife; a beer mug and a bottle of claret; a brown teapot and a cup and saucer; a milk jug and salt shaker; an old-fashioned tin of Arnott's Famous Biscuits and a fruit pie with a slice missing. An oil lamp is on the table too, with

Grandad's pipe, a box of matches and a mess of playing cards. The brown wooden table has two matching chairs. An open dresser top displays a blue patterned dinner service and bowls of eggs and fruit. The drawer has cutlery in one side and in the other there is a conglomeration of spare keys, buttons, pencils, pliers and hammer, serviettes in rings, a block of chocolate and a packet of envelopes. In the cupboard underneath are the old couple's Sunday-best things reserved for visitors — a pretty tea-tray, a plate of cakes, silver cheese dish, cruet set and sugar basin. On the very top of the dresser is a coffee pot, some correspondence and a spike file of insurance and rates notices and receipts that date back many years.

A flowering pot-plant and lace curtains brighten the window in the back wall of the kitchen and beneath these is the sink with its single brass tap and wooden draining board. A batch of scones has been put on the sink to cool and a bottle of fly spray is close by. Under the sink, behind a green curtain, is a box of fresh vegetables. Be careful that you don't trip over the wooden bucket or the floor mop or feather duster as we go over to the corner of the room to look at the old wind-up gramophone on a little white table. Nearby is the fuel stove set in a fireplace. A stew is cooking in a black-bottomed saucepan and the kettle is on. On the mantelpiece is a pretty blue enamelled cannister set, some wooden condiment jars and a wooden salt-box. Grannie's recipe book is there too, with all her favourite handwritten recipes.

While you are looking up at the chimney breast to admire Grandad's stuffed fish trophy and his old rifle, take care not to step on the poodle asleep

in his basket on the hearth, or on his dinner that is in a little dish marked 'Fido'. Near the stove is Grannie's food preparation bench. She must have forgotten she was making jam tarts because the dough has been rolled out with the wooden rolling pin and some circles of dough are already in the patty pan. A tin of strawberry jam has a jam-covered spoon standing in it. A mincing machine is clamped to the edge of the bench and a potholder hangs above. Under the bench is an old wooden fruit box filled with firewood for the stove and a scuttle full of coal.

The walls of the room, papered with old-fashioned yellow roses, are hung with a few ornaments — a framed poem 'To Mother'; an Irish proverb 'May the Good Lord take a liking to you, but not too soon'; a photo of Grandad when he was in the 1911 cricket team; a calendar and a hurricane lamp hanging on a hook. Over in the back corner of the room, fitted under the staircase, is the laundry where we can see a cement washtub and a cane basket filled with soiled linen. On the wall is a shelf with some tins of housepaint.

The door leading to the laundry has a couple of nails driven in to hang up Grannie's old straw sunhat and Fido's walking lead. We had better close the door, however, because there is a white chook peering into the kitchen! But don't move too quickly or you will bump your head on the parrot's cage hanging near the window. Now that the door has been moved we can see a pantry, well supplied with groceries.

Let us go upstairs. We have to pass the antique hallstand where Grandad's black silk umbrella and his walking stick are kept. On one of the hat hooks is his best grey felt hat. The wallpaper in the hallway is gold with white spots, and on the wall is a barometer and two framed pictures — one of a very buxom lady and the other of a horseless carriage. A grandfather clock and a picture of a sailing ship are at the top of the varnished stairs.

The bedroom is bright and cheerful. Unfortunately smoke has smudged the front of the little white fireplace — but the burning fire is nice, isn't it? On the mantelpiece is a white china vase hand-painted with pink and gold and filled with paper flowers. As well, there are two little portraits of some long-departed relatives. Blue floral paper covers the walls and blue-patterned lace is over the window. The floor covering is brown linoleum, brightened by a colourful hand-woven mat in front of the fireplace. A pair of red felt slippers are warming on the hearth near a small footstool, and an old-style clothes-horse is being used to dry a pair of bloomers, a singlet and Grandad's blue-striped socks. On top of the wardrobe is a hatbox containing Grannie's Sunday hat. The wardrobe itself is old-fashioned, with some coat-hangers inside. On an antique wash-stand are a water jug and basin with pink flowers painted on them. There is soap in the matching soap dish, and an alarm clock, shaving mug, brush and cut-throat razor. A towel is hanging on the side rail.

The bed is a big brass one with a thick mattress, sheets, a brown blanket and a multi-coloured bed-spread that has been hand-crocheted in tiny squares. Under the bed we can see a chamber pot that matches the wash-stand set. Next to the bed is a little round table, covered with a hand-made lace cloth, that holds the family Bible, an oval-framed picture of an old gentleman with long whiskers, and a candle in an enamel holder complete with a matchbox and spent matches. Because they could not fit on the table a couple of magazines and books lie on the floor. Among these is the family photograph album, filled with delightful old photos. There are more pictures on the walls — a gold-framed photo of Grandad and Grannie on their wedding day; Grandad in his World War One uniform; a little silver-framed picture of a woman and child; a set of framed miniatures of three babies; and Grandad's war medals in a frame. Over the wash-stand is a fancy gold cross that reads 'God loves you and so do I'; over the fireplace is a carved frame with a print of a country scene; and close by is a sentimental poem 'To Mum and Dad'. Someone has tucked a red rose behind the frame.

If we care to climb up through the manhole to the attic we shall see where the old people store items that they finished with long ago. A rocking horse keeps company with a discarded mattress. A very ornate perambulator stands empty and lonely. *Alice in Wonderland* and other old children's books, a butterfly net and a Japanese parasol are scattered around the floor. A suitcase, long unused, carries tattered labels from foreign places. In a dark corner is an antique rocking cradle. There is also an aged trunk full of Grannie's treasures: an evening fan, some jewellery, a bundle of love letters tied with ribbon, and some yellowed tissue paper containing her Edwardian wedding dress with its pearl-buttoned bodice.

It is time to leave the old people with their memories and we will just call goodbye to them as we close the front door. Leaving the home of the older generation, let us go a little further along and see where the younger generation goes to school.

The Schoolhouse

The schoolhouse has only one classroom because there are not very many children dolls. It is a pretty pastel pink building with scalloped woodwork, painted-on windows and a little garden. The roof is tall because it contains an attic where the teacher lives. Her room is furnished with a table and chair, carpet and a comfortable bed. The walls are covered with pink floral paper and some framed Australian prints. When it is time for the children to arrive for school she shuts the door behind her and goes down the stairway at the side of the building.

The front wall of the schoolhouse opens downwards to form a playground with a green lawn, and a path leading to the classroom where a bell hangs at the entrance. The entire interior is painted cream. Brown desks and seats for eight children take up the centre area and the teacher's desk and chair stand in one corner. Someone has put an apple on her desk. An upright piano and stool are in another corner, with a vase of flowers and some music on top. On the far wall is a blackboard, a clock and a chart explaining the origin of the primary products of Australia. Lots of colourful posters are on the walls too, along with a poem that reads:

> Teacher loves good girls and boys
> Of every age and level.
> But Teacher knows that every class
> Has its little devil.

And indeed, on a small shelf under the ceiling there really is a tiny red fur devil who no doubt inspires a little naughtiness in the class now and again. On a lower shelf a plastic tank is kept for nature-study lessons. In here, among some pebbles, lives a tiny green frog with big rolling eyes. Of course there is a packet of frog food for him. In the cupboard are workbooks for each of the children on eight different subjects such as Spelling, Writing and Poetry, and class scrapbooks on projects such as Space Travel, Wild Animals and School Sports Photographs. As well, there are boxes of jigsaws, sewing, weaving, number blocks for teaching simple sums, spare chalk and pencils, a bead counting toy and a clock for learning how to tell the time.

We are getting a little short of time ourselves and the shopping centre has yet to be seen. Luckily it isn't far away from the school.

41

Rainbow Arcade

Rainbow Arcade is a small complex of shops in a white three-storied building that is painted in simulated blocks with black trimming. Each of the shops has its own individually coloured brickwork, and the name of the business is painted over each door.

The Greengrocer, whose shop is naturally painted green, has a display of choice fruit and vegetables behind the glass window. He is a lively Italian gentleman with a bright smile, black hair and moustache, and is sporting a red tartan T-shirt under his black coat. On the counter top is a pair of scales and a pumpkin that has just been cut into pieces. There is a good selection of apples, oranges, pears, bananas, potatoes, carrots, lettuce and pineapples. In red net bags hanging on the wall are some specially priced local apples, oranges and potatoes. Set up on a stand outside the shop are today's specials of strawberries, grapes and cauliflowers. A sign on the wall says that the shop is open until 5pm on Saturdays, which is handy to know.

The Grocer's Shop is bright yellow and its window is filled with all kinds of groceries from cordials to chutney. The grocer himself is a tall, sad-looking man who is beginning to lose his hair. He is neatly dressed in a blue striped shirt, yellow tie and white apron. In the counter front are various loaves of bread, bottles of milk, jam tarts, pies, and cakes such as cherry, chocolate, Swiss roll and rich fruit cake. There is also a selection of cheese. It is obvious that one cheese has been slightly gnawed by a mouse! Let's be polite and pretend that we cannot see the little grey mouse sitting quietly on a ledge in the top of the shop. There is a wonderful variety of confectionery — popular brands of block and boxed chocolates and old favourites like Mars Bars, Crumble Bars, Crunchies, Kit Kats and packets of Pascall sweets. A display stand holds a choice of packeted biscuits. On the back wall are all the grocery lines — soap powder, baby needs, breakfast foods, tinned fruits, juices, sugar, tea, coffee, shoe polish, dog food and so on. Fresh farm eggs are also available. For the children there are toffee apples, gingerbread men and some colourful sweets in a tall glass jar on the counter. When the grocer rings up the cash register we can see that there is quite a lot of money already in the till, so business must be good!

Next door is *The Ice-cream Shop* which has pink roll-down shutters that are padlocked when the shop is closed — perhaps ice-cream burglars are bad in this area! However, the shop is open now and it is a bright and cheerful place with vivid striped, starred and spotted wallpaper and a scalloped canopy. The pleasant lady behind the counter offers a choice of twelve flavours of ice-cream but it is very difficult to decide between so many. They are set out in rows and are labelled choc-chip, strawberry, coconut, toffee, caramel and so on. And in case we are further tempted, there are also some foil-wrapped chocolate eggs for sale.

The bus stop is just outside, and a useful time-table is pasted on the wall.

The white-tiled place is *The Butcher Shop*, and the window has an interesting display of meat available for bulk-buying. The butcher is pleased to see us. He is a very outgoing fellow with untidy brown hair, white coat, red bow tie and blue striped apron. The meat looks quite good — nice legs of lamb, rolled beef roast, minced steak, sausages, lamb chops and even fresh fish. Some more sausages hang on one of the hooks of the rail at the back of the shop. The butcher has a very business-like meat chopper and knife on the counter beside him. Advertisements of the weekly specials are written on the wall. A wooden chopping block stands in the corner and a clock hangs over the door of the freezer room.

There are more shops on the next level, which can be reached by stairs painted on the shopping

complex wall. The first we come to is the yellow-fronted *Toy and Book Shop*. Christmas must be approaching because the window is stacked with toys of all kinds and a notice suggests that we 'lay-by now'. Such a kindly old lady runs the shop. She has grey hair in a bun, a fawn-patterned dress with a lace scarf, and a pearl brooch. Books for sale fill two shelves and they all look interesting. Among the toys are skateboards, small metal cars, fur animals, boxed games, a cuddly koala and baby dolls in lace bonnets. On the counter is a box of gift cards for all occasions. A Christmas tree is for sale, too, and best of all is a large bin of tiny toys available at bargain prices.

Next door is *The Boutique*, a very feminine, pink-painted shop with a little bricked-in garden of flowers and a window showing some lovely summer party dresses. We can see that they will accept Bankcard. The proprietress is standing in the back of the shop with one hand on her hip, watching for customers, and with a very determined look in her eye. She is smartly dressed in a white blouse, gold necklace and navy silk skirt. The salon is luxuriously decorated with pink floral foil wallpaper and a beige plush carpet. Everything looks expensive. Fancy shoes — some decorated with diamantes — stand on little tables. There are necklaces of jet beads, pearls, coloured glass and gold chain, and a brass stand of gaily coloured umbrellas. One can choose from a box of scarves, and it would take ages to try on all the hats! They are arranged on millinery stands — hats of straw, fabric, lace and velvet, embellished with

frills, lace, braid or feathers. A round silver-framed mirror is over the hat table, and a full-length mirror is attached to the wall next to the fitting room. Some elegant hat boxes are on an overhead shelf. Just look at these exclusive dresses! There are day dresses, evening dresses, sundresses and party dresses in many colours and fabrics. Some have lace or flower trimming. There is an ocelot fur coat, a beautiful wedding dress of white lace with a two-tiered skirt, and a pink lace bridesmaid's dress to go with it. They all hang on wooden coat-hangers on full display, but there isn't a price ticket in sight. Thank goodness for Bankcard!

The only remaining place on this level is *The Doctor's Surgery*. As we are all quite well we fortunately don't need his services, but perhaps we could just peep through the lace-curtained window and see inside. It is all clinically white except for the blue carpet. There are some ornaments on the walls: a picture of a country scene with horses; illustrations of anatomy; a clock; a letter-rack; a red sign saying 'Warning — smoking is a health hazard'; and a white sign saying 'Patients must register house calls before 8am'. The doctor is conventionally dressed in shirt, tie and trousers with a white coat. Naturally he has a stethoscope around his neck. He has a very kind face and receding grey hair, and is occupied at the moment with writing prescriptions. The desk is cluttered with a blotting pad, telephone, pen, receipt book and Mrs Dolly's X-rays. The examination couch, with its white pillow and sheet, looks too sterile to be comfortable. Above the white sink at the back wall is a shelf of medicine bottles containing cough balsam, antiseptic, vitamins, Senokot and other medicines, and some packages of Disprin, cotton-wool, bandages and Deepheat. If the doctor needs to check up on symptoms or medical tests he has only to look up his reference books on the shelf near his desk. There are no patients waiting to see him at the moment, but three white chairs are provided, and there are magazines in a holder for patients who are sometimes kept waiting.

Have you any letters to post? There is a red post-box on this level. A notice on the wall here

says 'For all sewing purposes visit the Attic Dressmaker', and another notice says 'Upstairs to Arcadia Cafe for delicious meals'. We could surely do with a cup of tea, so let us go up.

It is difficult to go past *The Attic Dressmaker's Shop* and not stop to buy something. She has a good stock of materials, including wool tweeds, Swiss cottons, corduroys and printed georgettes. Paper patterns are available, too, in different brands. There is a wide range of colours in sewing cottons and a whole bin of lovely knitting wools. The dressmaker looks business-like with a tape-measure around her neck — perhaps we interrupted her work. In fact there is a length of

pink material laid out on the counter with a pattern and scissors on it, ready for cutting. She herself is smartly dressed in a stylish pink blouse and brown skirt, and her face is pleasant and framed in curly brown hair. It is only a small shop, with pink and green floral wallpaper and green velvet carpet, and just enough space to fit in a dressmaker's model, a spare chair and a treadle sewing machine, which seems to have an almost completed dress on it.

Arcadia Cafe has a lot to offer. What would you like? Just pick up a tray and collect whatever cups, plates and cutlery are needed, then make your selection. There are sandwiches, meat pie and vegetables, fish and chips, chop and vegetables, or sausages and eggs. For dessert you can have chocolate pudding, jelly, custard tart, pineapple meringue, ice-cream with strawberry sauce, or strawberry tart. Extra cream is available for 20 cents. And there are donuts, iced cakes or jam tarts. Would you prefer tea, coffee or a milkshake?

The little tables are painted red, green and yellow, and all have green checked tablecloths. While we eat we can admire the bright decor with its red awning and red and white striped wallpaper. Did you notice that they take Diners Card here? And did you see that lovely wedding cake on display? A notice says that they make them to order — this would be a very nice place to have a wedding reception, up on the top floor of Rainbow Arcade.

The lady behind the counter keeps smiling at us. She is very cheerful, and most attractive with her black hair, red floral dress and pretty white apron. The chef is probably her husband. He doesn't look so cheerful, in his glassed-in kitchen, rolling out the pastry. He has some pie apples and a bin of flour at hand. A curry is cooking in the saucepan on the stove and a chicken is roasting in the oven. The kitchen is well equipped with shining utensils hanging on the wall. The chef himself is dressed in a white coat and cap, and he has a droopy black moustache. He is probably grumpy because of the large pile of washing-up on the sink waiting to be done!

Well, I am afraid it is time to go. Let's walk down to the street together, and then we must say goodbye. We cannot stay forever in the world of make-believe, but it has been fun, hasn't it? Everyday life in the real world can be fun too, of course, if we can stay young in heart.

Making Furniture and Accessories

The Preliminaries

For making accessories you will need a small coping saw, craft knife, plastic set-square, pair of tweezers, scissors, darning needle and some fine sandpaper. Cut the sandpaper into small squares and make several sanding blocks from pieces of wood — one about 50 mm × 50 mm and another 25 mm × 12 mm. A round file is essential and can be made from a short length of sandpaper glued around a toothpick. For very close work a magnifying glass that hangs around the neck is handy, and can be purchased from a craft shop. A good investment would be a pen with gold permanent ink from a stationery store.

Materials required depend upon the accessories you are making. Basically you will need fast-drying acetate glue for wood and plastic and white glue for paper and fabric, dressmaking pins with large coloured plastic heads, wooden beads of various shapes and sizes, undercoat paint and the small tins of coloured paints suggested for painting the house with the addition of a tin of mid-brown and some timber-coloured antiquing paint. Hinges are almost impossible to find for use on miniature work, but the nylon hinges used for model aeroplane wing-flaps are the next best thing and are obtainable at hobby shops. Brass taps, hat hooks, door-plates and so on can be purchased, but with a little ingenuity can also be hand-made. Handles and knobs for drawers and doors can be found in the range of upholstery pins.

Many small accessories are made with the help of coloured advertising pictures from gift catalogues, magazines and brochures. The pictures must be suitably sized and in correct proportion to each other (Have you ever seen a tin of condensed milk larger than a packet of corn-flakes?), and the paper should be of reasonably good quality, or it will stain or fade.

If furniture fails to stand upright when it is put on the dollhouse carpet it may need more weight. Cut a small piece of a heavier wood and attach it in an unobtrusive place beneath the article. When using balsa wood for furniture-making this problem can be overcome if a little heavier wood is incorporated during the construction, say for a chair seat or table top.

Use guipure lace to produce 'carved' wood. This lace has a heavily raised pattern and is ideal for our purpose. Buy designs with individual flowers that are no larger than 8 mm in diameter. Cut out the flowers and perhaps a few leaves, saturate them with white glue and arrange them in a suitable design wherever needed. When it is thoroughly dry, undercoat and paint the article of furniture, including the lace, in the usual way.

Basic Design for Various Items

The following articles have the same method of construction, using 6.4 mm balsa or other timber if preferred. The basic requirements are:

    1 top piece (the width of the article)

    2 side pieces (the height of the article)

    1 bottom piece (the width less the thickness of the two sides)

    1 or more shelves (each the same size as the bottom piece)

    1 back piece (to fill in the back)

Use the following sequence to make each article:

1. Lay the bottom piece on the bench.

2. Stand a side piece at each end of the bottom piece.

3. Place the top piece on the top.

4. Insert the shelves.

5. Glue together all the connecting surfaces.

Variations: Doors and drawers may be simulated by gluing on a false front and adding a knob. Working doors can be made by cutting a door to fit the space and attaching it with hinges. Working drawers can be made by following instructions given for the Antique Dressing Table.

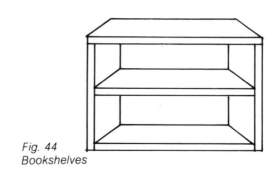

Fig. 44
Bookshelves

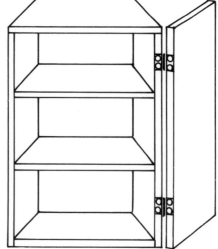

Fig. 45
Linen press

Simple Bookshelves

Suggested width 80 mm, height 70 mm, depth 20 mm (Fig. 44).

Linen Press or Cupboard

Suggested width 90 mm, height 130 mm, depth 40 mm. Add a door (Fig. 45).

Fig. 46
Bedside table

Bedside Table

Suggested width 50 mm, height 60 mm, depth 30 mm. Add a drawer and a straight pediment on the top at the back (Fig. 46).

Antique Bookcase

Suggested width 60 mm, height 70 mm, depth 20 mm. Carve the front edges of the side pieces before attaching. Carve a pediment and add to the top. Glue on lace trimming where required. Attach small wooden beads for feet (Fig. 47).

Fig. 47
Antique bookcase

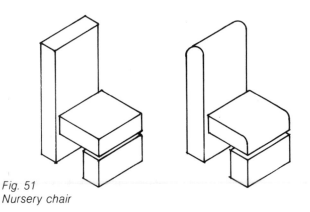

Fig. 48
Sideboard

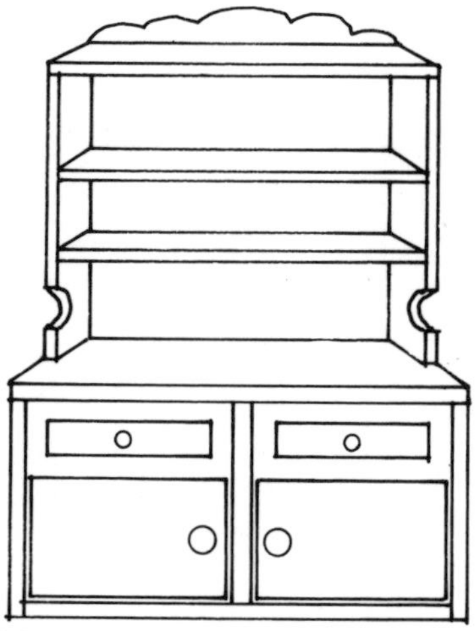

Fig. 49
Kitchen dresser

Fig. 50
Antique wardrobe

Fig. 51
Nursery chair

Sideboard

Suggested width 120 mm, height 70 mm, depth 40 mm. Add two doors. Carve a pediment and attach to the top. Door panelling may be added using 1.6 mm balsa. Add lace trimming where required. Add small wooden beads for feet and doorknobs (Fig. 47).

Kitchen Dresser

Top unit: suggested width 90 mm, height 65 mm, depth 25 mm. Low unit: suggested width 90 mm, height 65 mm, depth 45 mm. Make the dresser in two separate units. Add a simple pediment to the top, either at front or back. Add doors and drawers to the lower unit — these may open or be simulated. Add knobs of wood or metal (Fig. 49).

Antique Wardrobe

Suggested width 90 mm, height 140 mm, depth 40 mm. Add two doors. Add a carved pediment on top at the front. Put a hanging rod inside of 3 mm dowel with a dress eyelet at each end. Glue to the inside wall. The doors may be decorated with panelling, using 1.6 mm balsa, or may have full-length mirrors glued on. Plastic mirror is preferable to glass mirror because it weighs less. Add lace trimming, doorknobs and small sturdy feet (Fig. 50).

For a modern wardrobe do not add pediment, panelling or lace trimming.

Tables and Chairs

Nursery Chair

Chair back 1 piece 60 mm × 30 mm of 6.4 mm balsa or solid wood
Seat 1 piece 30 mm × 30 mm of 6.4 mm balsa or solid wood
Front leg 1 piece 30 mm × 15 mm of 6.4 mm balsa or solid wood

1. Glue the front leg under one edge of the seat.
2. Glue the seat to the back.
3. Sandpaper the front edge of the seat and the top of the back until they are nicely rounded.
4. Paint a bright colour (Fig. 51).

Kitchen Chair

Chair back   1 piece 48 mm × 30 mm of 6.4 mm balsa

Seat   1 piece 42 mm × 42 mm of 4.8 mm balsa

Back legs   2 lengths each 82 mm of 6.4 mm square wood

Front legs   2 lengths each 30 mm of 6.4 mm square wood

Leg rungs   2 lengths of 3 mm dowel

Seat supports   4 matchsticks

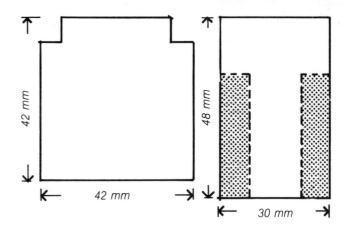

1. Cut a 6 mm square from each of the back corners of the seat.
2. Glue the front legs under the front corners of the seat.
3. Fit the back legs into the cut-out squares at the back of the seat and glue into position.
4. Cut matchsticks to fit all around under the seat, gluing to both the seat and the legs to give extra support.
5. Cut the rungs to fit neatly between the front and the back legs on each side of the chair.
6. Draw a design on the chair back as illustrated and cut it out. Transfer the remaining T-shape to the chair and glue it between the upper extensions of the back legs.
7. Using the round file, carve a fancy edge on the top railing.
8. Cut out two tiny triangles of balsa, glue them to the junction of the seat and the upper back legs, and when dry carve the upper edge slightly.
9. Paint the completed chair (Fig. 52).

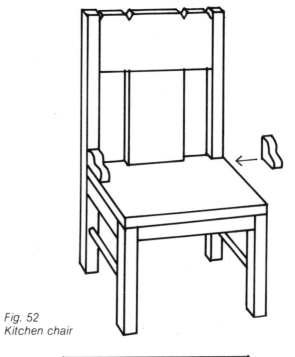

Fig. 52
Kitchen chair

Dining Chair

Sides   2 piece each 90 mm × 50 mm of 4.8 mm balsa, with the grain running lengthwise

Crest rail   1 piece 20 mm × 35 mm of 4.8 mm balsa

Seat   1 piece 35 mm × 35 mm of 6.4 mm balsa or heavier wood

Leg rungs   2 lengths each 32 mm of 3 mm dowel

Back rails   4 round wooden toothpicks cut to 35 mm length, with a wooden bead (5.5 mm diameter) threaded on each

1. Rule the chair sides into 10 mm squares and draw in the design illustrated. Cut them out and ensure that both sides are identical.
2. Draw the design on the top edge of the crest rail and carve it out, using the round file.

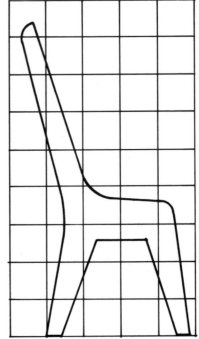

3. Glue the seat between the two sides.

4. Stand the toothpicks on the seat near the back edge so that the beads are only just touching each other. Mark where they are to be located on the seat and drill shallow holes. Glue the toothpicks in.

5. Drill corresponding holes under the crest rail and glue it on to the rails, gluing it at the same time to the chair sides.

6. Push the beads about three-quarters of the way up the rails in a neat row and glue them into place.

7. Join the legs with the rungs at the front and the back.

8. Glue lace trimming on the crest rail and allow to dry well.

9. Paint the chair.

10. Cut a piece of thin cardboard to fit the seat, cover it with fabric, folding under the edges, and glue it to the chair (Fig. 53).

Fig. 53
Dining chair

Lounge Chair

Back	1 piece 50 mm × 50 mm of 6.4 mm balsa
Arms	2 pieces 60 mm × 60 mm of 6.4 mm balsa
Seat	1 piece 45 mm × 40 mm of 6.4 mm balsa
Base	1 piece 50 mm × 60 mm of 12 mm solid wood (not balsa)
Upholstery	Stretch velvet; upholstery braid 12 mm wide; plastic foam 3 mm thick; plastic foam 6 mm thick
Feet	4 small wooden beads

1. Rule the arms into 10 mm squares, copy the design as illustrated and cut the arms out, making sure that both sides are identical (Fig. 54a).

2. Completely cover each arm with velvet, gluing the raw end of the fabric on one side where the shaded areas are illustrated (Fig. 54b).

3. Cover the back piece with velvet on one side and the edges only, folding over 6 mm to the uncovered side and gluing down.

4. Glue the back on to the base with the uncovered part facing the front of the chair.

5. Stand the two arms on the base, insides facing one another, and thinly glue where the sides meet the back edges and the base, ensuring that the back leans with the slope of the arms (Fig. 54c).

6. Cut a piece of thin cardboard and a piece of 3 mm plastic foam the same size as the back and glue them together. Cover the foam side with velvet, folding the material over to the back of the cardboard, and glue it down. Put some glue on the bare wood area of the chair back, press the cardboard into position and hold or peg it firmly until it dries.

7. From the balsa seat cut out the back corners so that the seat will fit neatly into the chair (Fig. 54d). Cut a piece of 6 mm plastic foam the same shape as the seat and glue the seat and foam together. Cover the foam side with velvet, taking it over the sides and gluing it just under the wood.

8. Put some glue in the base of the chair and press in the upholstered seat. Weigh it down until it dries.

9. Cut a piece of the upholstery braid so that it will fit around the base of the chair to meet neatly at the back and glue it down.

10. Attach the feet under each corner of the chair (Fig. 54e).

Lounge chair

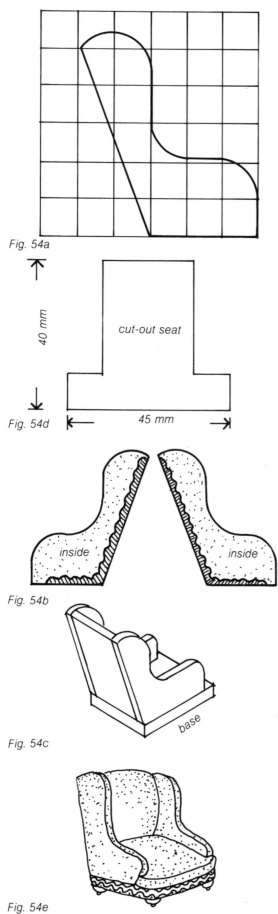

Fig. 54a

40 mm

cut-out seat

Fig. 54d ⟵ 45 mm ⟶

inside   inside

Fig. 54b

base

Fig. 54c

Fig. 54e

Nursery Table

Table top 1 piece 70 mm × 85 mm of 6.4 mm balsa
Legs   4 lengths each 30 mm of 10 mm dowel
1.   Slightly round off the edges of the table top with sandpaper.
2.   Glue a leg under each corner of the table top, 6 mm in from the edge.
3.   Paint the table a bright colour (Fig. 55).

Kitchen Table

Table top   1 piece 90 mm × 110 mm of 6 mm wood (not balsa)
Overlay   1 piece 95 mm × 115 mm of 1.6 mm balsa
Legs   4 lengths each 35 mm of 12 mm square wood
Leg support 220 mm of 6 mm square wood
1.   Glue the legs to the corners beneath the table top, keeping 6 mm in from the edges.
2.   Cut the leg support into pieces to fit closely under the table top between the legs and glue liberally to all surfaces.
3.   Hammer a panel pin through the table top into the top of each leg and countersink with a nail punch.
4.   Glue the overlay on top of the table.
5.   With a panel pin attach two small wooden beads on the end of each leg, gluing them securely.
6.   This style of table is suited to a scrubbed-paint finish (Fig. 56).

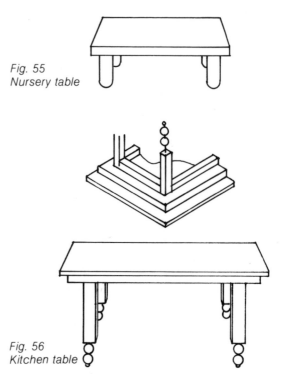

Fig. 55
Nursery table

Fig. 56
Kitchen table

Dining Table

Table top   1 piece 95 mm × 115 mm of 6 mm wood (not balsa)

Undertable 2 lengths each 91 mm of 6 mm square
support   wood
              2 lengths each 83 mm of 6 mm square
              wood

Legs   4 round wooden toothpicks and some wooden beads of various shapes (round, oval, long)

1. Very slightly round off the sharp edges of the table top.

2. Glue the supports under the table, keeping 6 mm from the edges, and forming a close-fitting framework.

3. To represent carved legs, thread wooden beads on each toothpick until they measure 50 mm. Glue each bead well as it is threaded. Make sure all the legs match. Securely glue the legs under the table top, snugly fitting them into the corners of the undertable support to give the necessary strength. Make sure that the legs are straight and even.

4. When the glue is perfectly dry, snip off the excess ends of the toothpicks. If the table does not stand evenly carefully sandpaper the uneven leg until remedied.

5. Sandpaper the table top until it is smooth and glossy. This style of table lends itself to teak-coloured antiquing paint and an attractive wood grain can be painted in very effectively (Fig. 57).

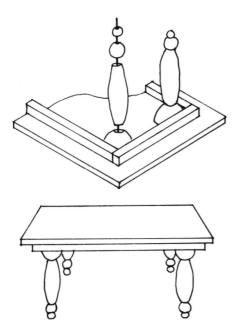

Fig. 57
Dining table

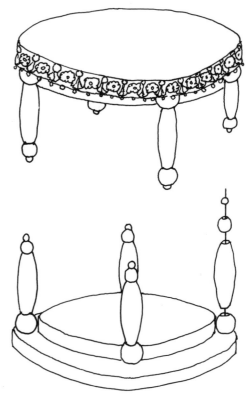

Fig. 58
Round occasional table

Round Occasional Table

Table top   1 circle 60 mm diameter of 6.4 mm balsa

Undertable An extra piece of 6.4 mm balsa
support

Legs   4 round wooden toothpicks and some wooden beads (long and round shapes)

Table edge A length of 6 mm wide guipure lace with a continuous pattern.

1. Drill four tiny holes under the table top exactly the same distance apart and 6 mm in from the edge.

2. Insert a toothpick into each hole and glue it well. Thread the beads on to the toothpicks, gluing each one. Each leg should measure 30 mm. Make sure that they are straight.

3. When the glue is quite dry, snip off the excess ends of the toothpicks.

4. For the undertable support cut a circle to fit under the table and to connect firmly with each leg. Glue it in securely and leave until dry.

5. Glue the lace around the edge of the table and allow to dry.

6. Paint or antique paint the completed table (Fig. 58).

The Fire and Fireplace

The Fireplace

Sides	2 pieces each 25 mm × 75 mm of 6.4 mm balsa
Top	1 piece 25 mm × 87.2 mm of 6.4 mm balsa
Bottom	1 piece 25 mm × 87.2 mm of 6.4 mm balsa
Mantel	1 piece 30 mm × 110 mm of 6.4 mm balsa
Hearth	1 piece 45 mm × 120 mm of 6.4 mm balsa
Frontpiece	1 piece 100 mm × 75 mm of 6.4 mm balsa
Inner wall	2 pieces each 25 mm × 62.2 mm of 6.4 mm balsa
Backpiece	1 piece 100 mm × 75 mm of 1.6 mm balsa
Extrusions	2 pieces each 106 mm of 3 mm square wood
	4 pieces each 26 mm of 3 mm square wood

1. Make a box of the sides, top, bottom and back as illustrated.

2. Line inside the back wall, side walls and floor, including the front step edge, with brick-patterned paper (available from a hobby shop).

3. Glue the inner wall pieces just inside the front edge of the box and cover the front and exposed edges with brick-patterned paper.

4. Cut the frontpiece out as illustrated.

5. Using a pencil, carefully measure and score down each side of the frontpiece as illustrated, pressing the pencil into the balsa sufficiently to indent the lines firmly. This decoration is optional.

6. With sandpaper slightly curve the front edge and the two side edges of the mantelpiece.

7. Paint the mantelpiece and the prepared frontpiece. White or timber-coloured paint would be suitable.

8. Glue the frontpiece to the front of the fireplace, then glue the mantelpiece to the top.

9. Glue the extrusions on — one just above the scored lines and the other immediately under the mantelpiece — taking them around the sides of the fireplace. Sandpaper the corners to a neat join, then paint them to match the mantelpiece.

10. Cover the top and edges of the hearth with brick-patterned paper, and glue it into position beneath the fireplace.

11. Glue adornments to the frontpiece. These can be made of gold bead capping, or small designs cut out of gold paper doily, or lace flowers glued on and painted gold (Fig. 59).

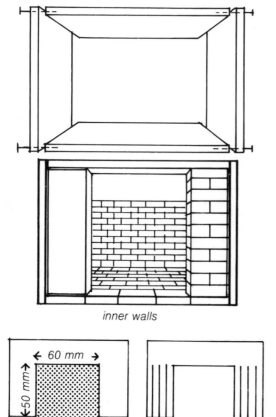

inner walls

← 60 mm →

50 mm

frontpiece

Fig. 59
Fireplace and fire

extrusions

The Fire

1. Gather some tiny pieces of dead wood about 5 mm diameter. These can be found on any twigs lying around the garden.
2. Cut them into lengths about 30 mm, leaving some jagged and with small offshoots protruding naturally.
3. With black crayon, colour most of the 'logs' black, but leave some 'unburned' ends. Use the crayon to smear 'smoke' on the back wall and floor of the fireplace with just a little on the side walls. Smooth the crayon and rub it in with the finger.
4. Pile the logs together into the fireplace just as you would for a real fire, but gluing them together as you go. Have some logs at cross-angles and scatter a few minute twigs around.
5. Take a small piece of bright red foil and cut it into jagged short lengths about 3 mm wide and tapering to a fine point. With the help of a pair of tweezers take each piece of foil, dip it in glue, and carefully insert into the spaces between the logs, with the pointed end upwards and the red side of the foil facing the front. Bend a few pieces over as flames appear to do when licking around wood. Tuck a little red foil around the lower logs to simulate embers. If properly placed the foil with catch the light and give an uncanny feeling of a cosy glowing fire in the dollhouse fireplace.
6. Save a few logs to keep on the hearth. Make a decorative wood-holder to put them in.

Bedroom Furniture

Suggested sizes:
double bed 160 mm × 100 mm
single bed   150 mm × 70 mm
child's bed 100 mm × 60 mm
Suggested materials:
base 12 mm balsa or other wood
ends 4.8 mm or 6.4 mm balsa

Modern Bed

Size of base As above for double, single or child size
Headboard 100 mm high by the same width as the base
Footboard 50 mm high by the same width as the base

1. Measure 25 mm up from the bottom of the headboard and attach the base with glue and panel pins. Keeping the base horizontal, attach the footboard in the same manner.
2. To strengthen, cut two lengths of 6 mm quarter-round moulding or 6 mm square wood, and glue under the base at each end.
3. Slightly round off the top corners of the head and footboards.
4. Paint the finished article (Fig. 60).

Antique Bed

Size of base As above for double, single or child size
Headboard 75 mm high by the same width as the base
Footboard 25 mm high by the same width as the base

1. Have the bottom edges of the headboard and footboard level with the bottom edge of the base. Attach with glue and panel pins.
2. Draw a carved design on the top of the headboard and file it out. Make a more simple design on the footboard.
3. Add lace decorations.
4. Insert plastic-headed pins through one or two small wooden beads and push into each top corner of the headboard with a little glue.
5. Insert panel pins through two wooden beads and make legs under the four corners of the base. Glue them well.
6. Paint the finished bed (Fig. 61).

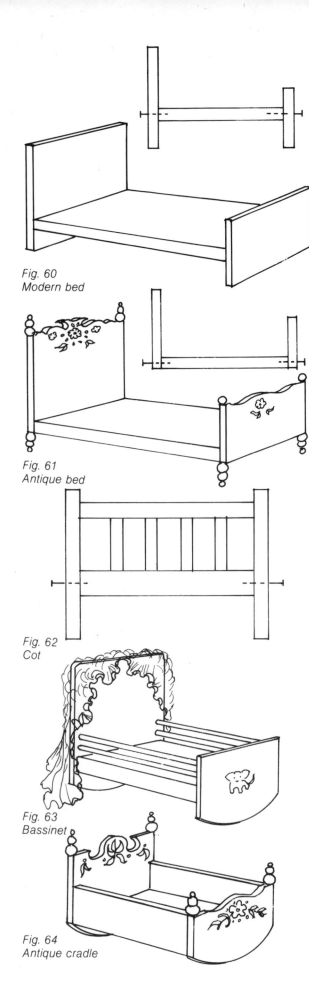

Fig. 60
Modern bed

Fig. 61
Antique bed

Fig. 62
Cot

Fig. 63
Bassinet

Fig. 64
Antique cradle

Cot for Toddler

Base   75 mm × 55 mm of 6.4 mm balsa
Headboard 55 mm × 55 mm of 6.4 mm balsa
Footboard 55 mm × 55 mm of 6.4 mm balsa
Side posts 8 lengths each 20 mm of 6 mm square wood
Top rails 2 lengths each 75 mm of 6 mm square wood

1. Measure 15 mm up from the bottom ends of the head and footboards and attach the base with glue and panel pins.
2. Glue four posts in upright positions on each side of the cot, spaced evenly apart.
3. Glue the top rails over the posts, and glue where the rails meet the bed ends.
4. Paint white or pastel and, when dry, glue on a small nursery motif (Fig. 62).

Bassinet

Base   55 mm × 40 mm of 4.8 mm or 6.4 mm balsa
Headboard 70 mm × 40 mm of 4.8 mm or 6.4 mm balsa
Footboard 45 mm × 40 mm of 4.8 mm or 6.4 mm balsa
Side rails 4 lengths each 57 mm of 3 mm dowel

1. Measure 15 mm up from the bottom of the end boards and attach the base with glue.
2. Place two side rails on each side of the bassinet, indenting each end 1 mm into the head and footboards and adding glue.
3. With sandpaper, curve the bottom of the bed ends slightly so that the bassinet will rock a little (but not too much or baby will tip out!).
4. Paint white or pastel and, when dry, glue on a small nursery motif.
5. Drape a length of fancy lace around the bedhead, allowing it to reach the floor each side and catching it back with tiny ribbons (Fig. 63).

Antique Cradle

Make this in the same way as the bassinet but with only half the height. Fill in the sides in lieu of railings. Carve and decorate the end boards lavishly. Paint it dark brown (Fig. 64).

Antique Dressing Table

Back	1 piece 130 mm × 80 mm of 4.8 mm balsa
Sides	2 pieces 45 mm × 35 mm of 4.8 mm balsa
Top	1 piece 85 mm × 40 mm of 6.4 mm wood (not balsa)
Drawer supports	3 lengths each 70.4 mm of 5 mm square wood
	4 lengths each 30 mm of 5 mm square wood
Mirror	Not larger than 65 mm × 65 mm

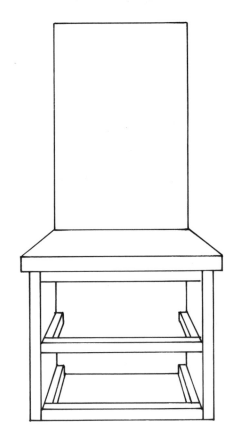

1. Join the two sides to the back, level at the floor and with the edges meeting.
2. Glue the top on.
3. Glue in the drawer supports, one at floor level, one under the top, and one exactly halfway between.
4. Mark in where the mirror will eventually be fitted and draw a design around that area, adding lace flowers and leaves.
5. Carve out a fancy design along the top edge of the back.
6. Add wooden beads with pins and glue to the top back corners. Pin and glue more beads under the dressing table for small feet.
7. If drawers are to be simulated, cut out two pieces of 4.8 mm balsa to cover the spaces, decorate them to match the back, and glue them into place.
8. If you are making the two drawers you will require:

Base	2 pieces 60 mm × 30 mm of 1.6 mm balsa
Side	4 pieces 25 mm × 10 mm of 1.6 mm balsa
Back	2 pieces 58 mm × 10 mm of 1.6 mm balsa
Front	2 pieces 58 mm × 10 mm of 1.6 mm balsa
Front facing	2 pieces 70 mm × 18 mm of 6.4 mm balsa

9. Stand the front, back and sides on edge and glue on to the edge of the base to form a box. Glue the front facing to the front of the box, centring evenly.
10. Add lace decorations to the front facings.
11. Paint the dressing table and, when dry, glue the mirror into position. Add gold upholstery pins for drawer handles (Fig. 65).

Note: A chest of drawers may be made in the same way as the dressing table but without the high back and the mirror.

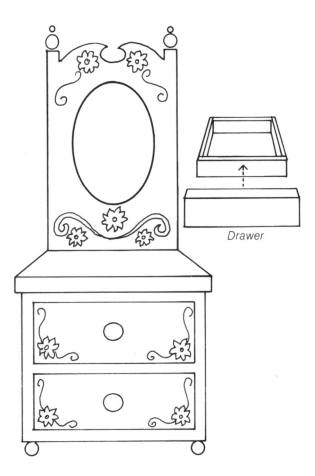

Drawer

Fig. 65
Antique dressing table

Vanity Table

Sides　　2 pieces 50 mm × 30 mm of 6.4 mm balsa or other wood

Top　　1 piece 70 mm × 40 mm of 6.4 mm balsa or other wood

Front panel　1 piece 45 mm × 10 mm of 6.4 mm balsa or other wood

Drape　　Lace or fabric 30 mm wide × approx. 230 mm long

1. Draw a slight kidney-shape on the front edge of the top and cut it out. Sandpaper it until smooth and even.
2. Glue the sides under the top and fit in the front panel.
3. If feet are required add small wooden beads. Paint the vanity table and allow to dry.
4. Gather one long edge of the drape, place it across the front panel and around the sides, and secure with glue. Cover the glued area with a length of daisy braid or lace (Fig. 66).

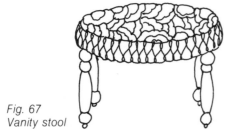

Fig. 66
Vanity table

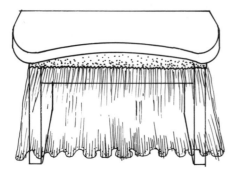

Fig. 67
Vanity stool

Vanity Stool

1. Cut an oval shape about 50 mm × 25 mm of 6.4 mm balsa.
2. Drill four holes and in each one insert a fancy cocktail stick (or toothpick threaded with beads) — finished length 25 mm.
3. Upholster the seat top with thin plastic

foam and fabric, gluing the fabric edges to the sides of the wood.
4. Cover the glued wood sides with daisy braid or lace (Fig. 67).

Other Furniture

Television Set

1. Using 6.4 mm balsa, make a box 50 mm wide × 30 mm high × 25 mm deep.
2. Paint it brown.
3. From a brochure on television sets find an attractive picture of a suitable size. Cut out the entire screen and glue it on to the box front.
4. Find a picture of suitably sized controls and glue that on as well. Otherwise use tiny pin or tack heads for a three-dimensional effect.
5. The set is made to sit on a shelf but if you prefer you could make a small table or a set of legs for it to stand on (Fig. 68).

Fig. 68
Television set

Footstool

1. Cut a circle 30 mm diameter from 12 mm balsa.
2. On top of this glue 3 mm plastic foam cut to the same size.
3. Cover the foam with fabric, gluing the edges around the sides of the wood.
4. Cut a length of 12 mm wide upholstery braid and glue it around the wood to cover the glued edges.
5. Push four plastic-topped pins through wooden beads and into the balsa to form small legs about 5 mm high (Fig. 69).

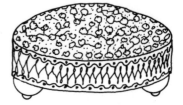

Fig. 69
Footstool

Wall Shelf (for recipe books etc.)

Ends 2 pieces 20 mm × 30 mm of 6.4 mm balsa
Shelf 1 piece of 6.4 mm balsa, 20 mm wide by
whatever length is needed

1. Mark the ends into 10 mm squares and draw in the pattern illustrated. Cut them out and smooth with sandpaper.
2. Glue the shelf between the ends.
3. Paint the wall shelf and, when it is dry, glue it to the wall in the dollhouse (Fig. 70).

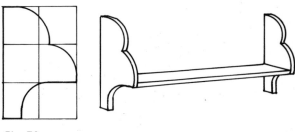

Fig. 70
Wall Shelf

Nursery Needs

Rocking Horse

Sides 2 pieces 70 mm × 50 mm of 4.8 mm balsa
Back 1 piece 20 mm × 25 mm of 4.8 mm balsa
Seat 1 piece 20 mm × 15 mm of 4.8 mm balsa
Handle 1 length 20 mm of 3 mm dowel

1. Rule the sides into 10 mm squares and copy the design as illustrated. Cut it out and smooth with sandpaper.
2. Paint the seat and back green, and the sides and handle white.
3. Glue the edge of the seat to the centre of the back as shown in the illustration.
4. Glue the joined seat and back in between the sides with the top of the back level with the top of the horse.
5. Glue the handle between the sides near the head of the horse.
6. Sketch in the outline of the lower part of the horse and legs, and paint all the area below this in green.
7. If there is any difficulty in balancing the rocker, add a small piece of heavier wood under the seat to tilt it either slightly forward or backward.
8. Paint in the eyes, spots, mane, bridle and saddle in black, and the saddle cloth in red (Fig. 71).

Fig. 71
Rocking horse

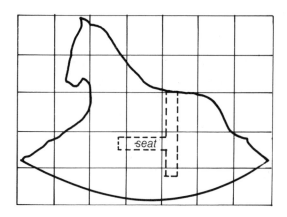

Doll's Pram

Sides   2 pieces 50 mm × 40 mm of 4.8 mm balsa
Top   1 piece 20 mm × 20 mm of 4.8 mm balsa
Back   1 piece 20 mm × 35 mm of 4.8 mm balsa
Foot   1 piece 20 mm × 20 mm of 4.8 mm balsa
Bottom 1 piece 20 mm × 40 mm of 4.8 mm balsa
Wheels 4 circles 12 mm diameter of 4.8 mm balsa
Handles 80 mm × 20 gauge wire

1. From each side cut out a corner measuring 30 mm × 20 mm.
2. Fit the top, back, foot and bottom pieces between the sides as illustrated and glue them into position.
3. With coarse sandpaper shape the back of the hood and the two bottom ends of the body as illustrated.
4. Bend the wire into a wide U-shape to form the handle, and push the ends into the top edges of the pram, adding a little glue.
5. Paint the pram pink or blue and paint the wheels black.
6. When the paint is dry glue the wheels into place, and put a gold upholstery pin in the centre of each one.
7. Paint a fine black line around the base of the hood.
8. Make a tiny blanket and pillow and put them into the pram (Fig. 72).

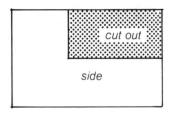

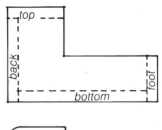

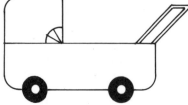

Fig. 72
Doll's pram

Fig. 73
Baby doll

Baby Doll

Head and body 2 pink plastic beads, size 12 mm
Arms   1 pink pipecleaner
Dress   75 mm of 40 mm wide broderie anglaise
Bonnet   A scrap of 12 mm wide lace

1. Join the two beads together with cotton that is knotted and glued tightly at each end.
2. Wrap the pipecleaner around the junction of the two beads, pull it tightly, and cut off each end to leave arms 12 mm long. Bend these forward slightly.
3. Fold over the raw edge of the broderie anglaise narrowly and machine stitch along the edge. Gather this and pull it securely around the neck of the doll, leaving the arms free above.
4. Form a tiny bonnet from the scrap of lace, gathering it along one edge and tying with a knot at the back of the head. Glue it to the doll.
5. With fine felt pens make black dots for eyes and a red dot for a mouth (Fig. 73).

Quoits

1. Cut a circle 25 mm diameter from 6.4 mm wood.
2. Drill a hole in the centre and glue in a 30 mm length of 3 mm dowel.
3. Paint it a bright colour.
4. Purchase six 12 mm brass curtain rings and loop them on to the upright dowel (Fig. 74).

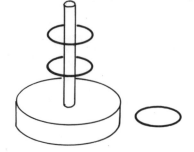

Fig. 74
Quoits

Toy Train

Base   1 piece 40 mm × 12 mm of 6.4 mm balsa
Boiler 1 length 25 mm of 12 mm dowel
Cabin   1 length 15 mm of 12 mm square balsa
Roof   1 piece 15 mm × 20 mm of 4.8 mm balsa
Funnels 2 lengths 10 mm of 3 mm dowel
Wheels 2 circles 15 mm diameter of 3.2 mm balsa
           4 circles 10 mm diameter of 3.2 mm balsa

1. Glue the boiler on top of the base, 3 mm back from the front edge.
2. Glue the cabin immediately behind the boiler.
3. Glue the roof on to the cabin.
4. Glue the wheels on, the larger wheels alongside the cabin, the smaller alongside the boiler.
5. Drill two holes on top of the boiler and glue in the funnels.
6. Paint the roof red, the wheels and the tops of the funnels black. Use a black felt pen to draw in cabin windows (Fig. 75).

Counting Beads

Base   1 piece 35 mm × 15 mm of 6 mm solid wood
Uprights 2 lengths 25 mm of 3 mm square wood
Wires 2 lengths 29 mm of 20 gauge wire
Beads A number of brightly coloured beads with large holes

1. Drill a hole at each end of the base, 3 mm from the edge.
2. Sharpen one end of each of the uprights and glue them in.
3. Paint the article in a bright colour.
4. Drill very tiny holes in each of the uprights near the top and halfway down.
5. Thread some beads on the wires, leaving enough space for them to move along with ease, and insert the wires into the holes drilled in the uprights. Glue them securely (Fig. 76).

'Learning the Time' Clock

Base   1 piece 35 mm × 25 mm of 4.8 mm balsa
Upright 1 piece 25 mm × 25 mm of 4.8 mm balsa

1. Glue the upright on edge in the centre of the base.
2. Paint the article a bright colour.
3. Draw a circle on the face of the upright with a fine black felt pen and clearly mark in the numbers of a clock.
4. Take a large paper fastener and cut off the 'legs', making one shorter than the other. Punch a hole in the square end of each one. These now become the hands of the clock.
5. Pin the hands to the centre of the clock with a small gold upholstery pin, leaving just enough slack for the hands to be moved (Fig. 77).

Fig. 75
Toy train

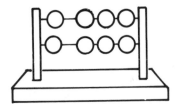

Fig. 76
Counting beads

Fig. 77
Learning clock

Accessories and Extras

Christmas Tree

1. Snip an end from a life-size plastic Christmas tree, about 75–100 mm in length.
2. Find a solid bottle top (such as comes on antiseptic bottles) and paint it black.
3. Fill the bottle top with dampened plaster of paris and immediately push in the trunk of the tree, making sure it is straight. Leave until the plaster has firmly set.
4. Paint the surface of the plaster brown.
5. Glue a little glitter on the tree (or use finely cut tinsel) and put some tiny wrapped packages around the base (Fig. 78).

Parrot Cage

Base and top	2 circles 30 mm diameter of 6.4 mm balsa
Bars	8 round wooden toothpicks cut to 40 mm length
Perch	55 mm of 20 gauge wire
Parrot	See instructions in section 'Modelling Plastic'

1. Paint the base and top red or green and, when dry, drill eight small holes evenly spaced around the perimeter of both, 3 mm in from the edge.
2. Bend the perch wire into a U-shape, having the bottom of the perch no more than 15 mm across. Push the ends of the wire into one of the circles as illustrated and add some glue.
3. Glue the parrot firmly to the perch, using a piece of fuse wire to secure it if in doubt.
4. Glue the toothpicks into the holes, joining the top of the cage to the bottom.
5. Put a tiny screw eye in the top of the cage and hang it to the ceiling of the dollhouse with a length of jewellery chain (Fig. 79).

Note: If you think Polly might need a drink you could include a tiny upturned pill bottle top in the cage for a water bowl.

Dressmaker's Model

Body	1 piece 50 mm long of 25 mm square balsa
Base	1 circle 30 mm diameter of 6 mm wood (not balsa)
Stand	1 piece 62 mm long of 3 mm dowel

1. Using a craft knife, carve the shape of a female body from the neck to thigh, smoothly finishing it with fine sandpaper.
2. Drill a hole 12 mm deep in the base of the model and insert the stand with glue.
3. Insert with glue the lower end of the stand into the centre of the base.
4. Paint the entire article brown. If the model tips over too easily, glue a 25 mm metal washer underneath the base (Fig. 80).

Fig. 78
Christmas tree

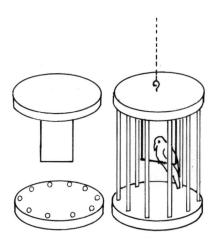

Fig. 79
Parrot cage

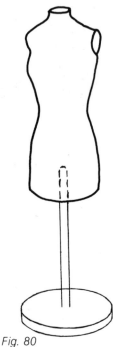

Fig. 80
Model

Umbrella

Stick 1 plastic cocktail stick cut to 80 mm
Ribs 6 lengths 50 mm of 20 gauge wire
Fabric 1 circle 100 mm diameter of thin non-fray fabric
Rib ends 6 tiny glass beads the same colour as the fabric

1. Lay the fabric flat and place the wires upon it, equal distance apart, with one end 3 mm from the centre and the other end 3 mm over the edge of the fabric.
2. Using glue sparingly, attach the wires to the fabric. Let dry.
3. Glue a bead on to the outside end of each wire.
4. Make a hole in the centre of the fabric, put a spot of glue on it and push the cocktail stick through so that it protrudes 6 mm. Carefully draw up the wires and fabric and roll them in one direction around the stick as you would roll a real umbrella.
5. Keep the umbrella furled by gluing a thread of the same colour around the centre.
6. Tie a piece of 6-strand embroidery cotton around the top of the handle, make a knot then fray out the ends to a tassle (Fig. 81).

Walking Stick

1. Cut a piece of 20 gauge wire to 75 mm length and bend the top over in the shape of a handle.
2. Bind the wire firmly with adhesive tape until it is well covered.
3. Paint the walking stick brown (Fig. 82).

Broom

1. Use the smallest size toothbrush (ideally the type used in electric toothbrush sets) and remove the handle.
2. Smooth the cut with sandpaper. Drill a hole in the top centre.
3. Insert the end of a 50 mm length of 3 mm dowel into the hole and glue it well.
4. Place a dress eyelet on to the dowel and glue it thoroughly where it meets the broom head.
5. Paint the handle the same colour as the broom (Fig. 83).

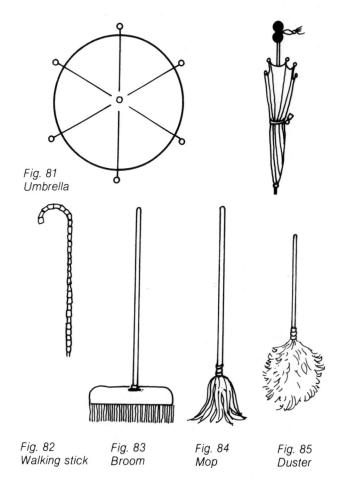

Fig. 81
Umbrella

Fig. 82   Fig. 83   Fig. 84   Fig. 85
Walking stick Broom   Mop   Duster

Mop

1. Cut a few strands from a real floor mop (or dishwashing mop) about 40 mm in length.
2. Bunch them around the end of a 50 mm length of 3 mm dowel and glue them well together. Bind the join very tightly with adhesive tape, then slide a dress eyelet down over the tape and glue it as well. Allow it all to dry.
3. Paint the handle and trim the mop ends to about 25 mm (Fig. 84).

Duster

1. Take a few very soft feathers from a real feather duster and glue them to the end of a round wooden toothpick that has been cut to 40 mm.
2. Bind the join carefully with black cotton, then smear glue over the cotton and allow to dry.
3. Paint the handle and trim the feathers to about 20 mm (Fig. 85).

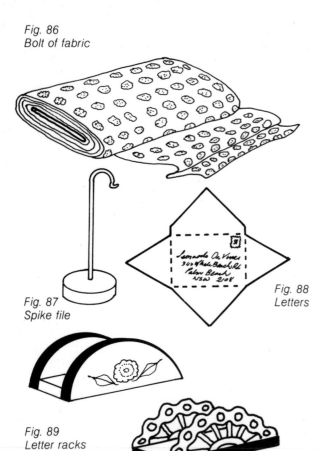

Fig. 86
Bolt of fabric

Fig. 87
Spike file

Fig. 88
Letters

Fig. 89
Letter racks

Letters

Make the envelopes by drawing a design as illustrated and folding it on the dotted lines. Slip a small piece of paper inside before sealing it to give the appearance of holding a letter. Cut a piece from a used stamp to make a tiny stamp on the corner of the envelope, and with a fine pen write a name and address. Draw a dotted cancellation mark over part of the stamp. The finished article should measure about 15 mm × 12 mm (Fig. 88).

Letter Rack

Base 1 piece 15 mm × 10 mm of 3.2 mm balsa
Sides 2 necklace ends, bead caps or other jewellery scraps
1. Paint the base black.
2. Glue the jewellery pieces on each side. If you cannot find any suitable jewellery, use 3.2 mm balsa instead. Cut it to shape as in the illustration, paint it black and glue on a flat-backed rhinestone or an attractive picture. Put the correspondence into the holder and stand it on a table or mantelpiece (Fig. 89).

Gift Cards

These can be arranged along the dollhouse mantelpiece at Christmas time or on a birthday. If children are playing at dollhouses they could 'post' them to each other. Most gift catalogues have pictures of cards they sell, as do advertisements. Cut out the small pictures of the cards, usually about 20 mm × 12 mm, and glue each one on to the light cardboard. Inscribe messages on the backs if you wish.

Paper Patterns

Make these in the same way as the gift cards but instead of cardboard make an envelope to glue them on. Put paper inside to make them a little bulky, and put them near the dollhouse sewing machine.

Bolts of Fabric (for a dollhouse shop)

Cut strips of dress material 50 mm wide × 150 mm long and roll them on to pieces of 4.8 mm balsa cut to 50 mm × 20 mm. The name of the fabric can be printed on the end of the wood. If possible use non-fraying materials (Fig. 86).

Spike File

Cut a 12 mm diameter circle from 6.4 mm balsa. Cut a 40 mm length of 20 gauge wire and bend the top over gracefully. Round-nosed plyers are handy for this. Push the wire into the centre of the wood, add a spot of glue, and the file is completed.

For tiny receipts, invoices, rates notices and so on, search among your own papers and you will be pleasantly surprised how many have miniature print incorporated in their letterheads. Cut them approximately 12 mm × 20 mm and vary the sizes a little. Put a few little signatures on some, add a date here and there, suggest that some might be final notices just for reality. Admittedly your personal papers will look a little ragged when you have finished (Fig. 87).

Candle Holders

Three types of candle holders are illustrated. The one shown in Fig. 90a requires a gold bead cap; a clear plastic mapping pin with the pin removed; a gold dress eyelet; and a round wooden toothpick, painted white.

1. From the pointed end, cut the toothpick to 25 mm and glue it into the eyelet.
2. Glue the eyelet on to the narrow end of the mapping pin.
3. Glue the mapping pin to the rounded side of the bead cap.
4. Make a wick by touching the candle point with a black felt pen.

The candle holder in Fig. 90b requires a crystal bead 10 mm diameter; a silver or gold sequin; and a round wooden toothpick, painted white.

1. From the pointed end, cut the toothpick to 25 mm and glue it into the bead — it may have to be whittled to fit in.
2. Glue the sequin under the bead.
3. Blacken the wick with a black felt pen.

The candle holder in Fig. 90c requires a dress eyelet; a round wooden toothpick, painted white; a metal earring back with threaded post removed; and a saucer from a miniature teaset or a thin shallow button 20 mm diameter.

1. Glue the eyelet to the centre of the saucer and paint both white.
2. Bend the earring back to fit tightly over the edge of the saucer, and glue it on to form the handle.
3. Paint the handle, the rim of the saucer and the top of the eyelet in blue.
4. From the pointed end of the toothpick, cut to 20 mm and glue it into the eyelet.
5. Melt a real candle and drip a little of the wax down the side of the toothpick. Blacken the wick with a black felt pen.
6. Cut three slivers of balsa about 6 mm long, blacken one end of each, and glue these 'spent' matches into the saucer.
7. Make a box of matches and glue this to the saucer.

Box of Matches

1. Cut a piece of 3.2 mm balsa 6 mm long × 4 mm wide.
2. Cover the top of the box with patterned paper.
3. Paint the short ends blue and the striking sides black.

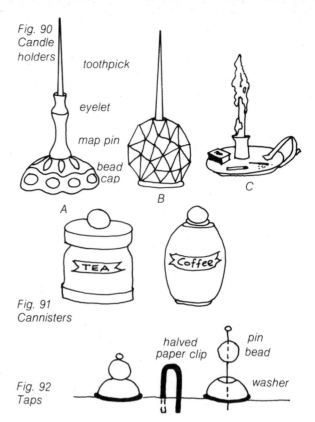

Fig. 90 Candle holders

toothpick
eyelet
map pin
bead cap

A B C

Fig. 91 Cannisters

TEA   Coffee

halved paper clip   pin bead
washer

Fig. 92 Taps

Cannisters for the Kitchen

Locate some wooden or plastic beads, square or barrel-shaped or oval, about 12 mm high. From your supply of advertisements find some clearly printed words 'sugar', 'tea' and 'coffee'. Cut these out neatly and glue one on each bead. Glue a tiny bead on the top for a knob. If necessary to define a lid, do so with a fine black pen. Some beads may have to be sandpapered flat at the bottom to prevent rolling (Fig. 91).

Tea Tray

Base 1 piece 45 mm × 30 mm of 3 mm balsa
Sides 4 matchsticks
Cut the matchsticks to fit neatly around the top edges of the base and glue them on. Paint the tray.

Taps

Miniature taps can be purchased, but you may prefer to make your own.

1. Lay a small chromed collar washer face down, put a coloured glass bead on top of it, and through these push a plastic-headed pin (red for hot water, green for cold).
2. A spout can be made from a paper clip cut to the right length and inserted into the back of the sink as illustrated (Fig. 92).

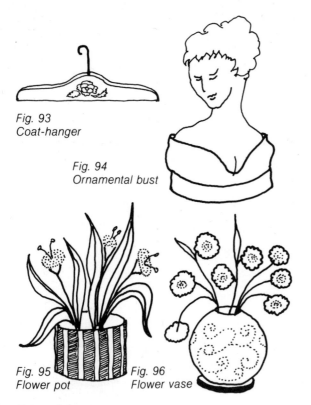

Fig. 93
Coat-hanger

Fig. 94
Ornamental bust

Fig. 95
Flower pot

Fig. 96
Flower vase

Coat-hangers

1. Cut 30 mm × 12 mm from 4.8 mm balsa. Draw the shape of the coat-hanger on this and file it out with sandpaper.
2. Paint the coat-hanger, then glue on a picture of a flower.
3. Cut 25 mm of 20 gauge wire and curve one end into a hook. Press the other end into the top of the coat-hanger and add some glue (Fig. 93).

Ornamental Busts and Statues

Buy a small plastic figure from a toyshop and saw it off at chest level. Glue this on to a piece of 6.4 mm balsa and, when the glue is dry, file the wood until it is the same shape as the bottom of the bust. Paint the entire article with undercoat and a final coat of white paint (Fig. 94).

A tiny whole figure can be mounted on a balsa block and used as a statue, and is most impressive if painted white to simulate marble.

A whole figure or bust can be mounted on a column carved from wood, painted white, and used to decorate an entrance hall or stairway.

Cut the head from a plastic stag, glue it to a thin circle of balsa and attach it to the wall over a fireplace. This suits a room with antique furniture. Leave the head unpainted.

Pots and Flowers

Pots for Plants

Use suitable small tops from bottles about 15 mm diameter for table or shelf use, and larger ones for floor tubs. Paint them bright colours.

Fill them with dampened plaster of paris and immediately insert the previously prepared plants. Allow to set before handling (Fig. 95).

Flower Vases

Sturdy plastic and glass beads make good vases if they have a large enough hole in the centre. Dip the end of each flower in glue before putting it into the vase, then arrange them nicely and allow the glue to dry.

If the vase is inclined to roll over, glue a large sequin or flattened bead cap underneath.

To make a vase particularly pretty, paint on a little design with a gold pen, using a series of heavy dots for best effect (Fig. 96).

Miniature Flowers

A spray of artificial flowers that is made up of tiny individual florets will, once taken apart, supply quite a few vases. Artificial flowers are quite easy to make and cost very little. You will require crepe paper and stamens.

To save expense, buy white crepe paper only. Cut a few pieces from the sheet and dye each a different colour with water-colour paints. Stamens can be bought from craft shops. Purchase one colour only, say pink, and dip the heads of some of them in different coloured oil paints, say red, black and yellow, to give a good variety.

Flower A: Chop coloured crepe paper with scissors into minute fragments. Dip the head of the stamen in glue and roll it in the chopped paper. For a larger sized flower allow this to dry then repeat the process. Finely chopped wool will also give good results. Allow the flowers to dry thoroughly before handling (Fig. 97a).

Flower B: Cut crepe paper circles 6 mm diameter in a variety of colours and insert a stamen through the centre, securing it with a spot of glue. These flowers are more attractive if petal shapes are indicated when cutting out the circles. Thin velvet or silk can be used instead of paper, but these

materials should be stiffened with fabric glue and allowed to dry before cutting out (Fig. 97b).
Flower C: Cut out crepe paper circles 6 mm and 12 mm diameter. With scissors slash these towards the centre, forming rough loose petals. Place a small circle on a large circle and insert a stamen through the centres of both, leaving the stamen head 12 mm above them. Put a little glue in the centre of the petals and roll them tightly around the stem. Fluff out the tops of the petals and allow to dry (Fig. 97c).

Leaves

A few green leaves should be included in the flower arrangements. Take several pieces of green crepe paper about 25 mm square. With scissors carefully cut strips about 3 mm wide and tapering to a fine point. Cut some leaves across the stretch of the paper and some running along the stretch — this gives some leaves that will stand upright and some that will curl over (Fig. 97d).

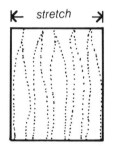

leaves

Bottles

Perfume Bottles

Use large glass or crystal beads with interesting shapes. Glue smaller matching beads on top for stoppers. Add labels from advertisements to identify the perfume or bath salts. If a bottle does not stand upright, glue a sequin underneath to give stability (Fig. 98a).

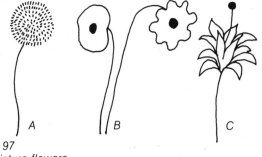

Fig. 97
Miniature flowers

Medicine and Confectionery Bottles

Tiny sample-size perfume bottles are ideal. Small glass phials that are used for certain medical inhalations are also suitable although they need to be filed smooth at the top and fitted with a glued-on bead stopper. However, as these are made of glass, small plastic pill bottles would be safer for young children. Whichever you use, add labels to explain the contents such as cough elixir, castor oil and so on.

Fill one or two of these bottles with sweets and stand them on a kitchen shelf. Sweets may be nonpariels or miniature squares of modelling plastic painted like licorice allsorts (Fig. 98b).

Wine and Sauce Bottles

These can be made from modelling plastic, or they can be carved from wood with a craft knife. As they are opaque, large wrap-around labels look best. Lids and tops can be suggested with a black pen (Fig. 98c).

Milk Bottles

Take a piece of ordinary white chalk about 25 mm long, shape it with a craft knife, sandpaper it smooth, and within a few minutes you will have a very presentable milk bottle. Glue on a tiny cap of gold or silver foil (Fig. 98d).

Baby's milk bottle is made in the same way, but should be slimmer and with a longer neck. When completed, paint the top area brown to represent the teat (Fig. 98e).

Fig. 98
Bottles

Frames, Pictures and Mirrors

Metal Frames

Realistic frames can be made from old brooches, fancy metal buckles, buttons with raised edges, pendants and earrings, some of which are very ornate. If a piece of jewellery has a stone set in it, simply gouge it out and glue the picture in its place. Some frames will have no backing for attaching the picture, as in the case of a buckle, but this can be remedied by cutting out a piece of cardboard, gluing the picture on, and fitting it into the frame.

Tiny round or square frames are often found in bracelet charms and these make excellent miniatures, particularly if displayed in groups, or if two or three are glued to a piece of velvet ribbon and hung on the wall.

When a frame is required to stand up on a table or mantelpiece, it will need a back support to assist it. If you cannot find any scraps of jewellery to suit the purpose, cut a small block of balsa, glue it to the back of the frame, and paint it silver or gold to match

Fig. 99
Metal frames

Wooden Frames

Modern pictures demand plain frames which may be no more than a rectangle of 3.2 mm balsa with space for the picture to be glued on it, allowing about 3 mm of the wood to show around the edges. These frames are best painted black.

To make a carved frame, cut out 3.2 mm balsa to the width of the frame you require, and make it as you would a real frame, with mitred corners. If these prove too difficult the corners could be cut square. Draw a design around the edges of the frame and carve it out gently with a round sandpaper file. Glue on lace decorations. When dry,

paint the frame brown. For further enhancement, touch up the lace with a little gold paste and burnish gently. To prepare the picture for this type of frame glue it on to a piece of white cardboard that is a little smaller than the overall size of the frame. Allow 3 mm of white to show around the picture when it is in the frame to serve as a mount (Fig. 100).

Fig. 100
Wooden frames

Pictures for Frames

The pictures that will hang in the dollhouse are most important. They can be little prints of the old masters or old Australian classics, portraits, photographs, or perhaps some hand-painted canvases of your own. Many suitable pictures can be found in magazines. An excellent source of quality pictures is in packets of foreign stamps. You may also wish to hang some of your family photographs that can be cut to fit the small frames, and these, especially children's photographs, create a personal point of interest.

Mirrors for Frames

These are usually found in compacts and old handbags, or they can be purchased cheaply in a chain store. At extra cost, mirrors can be cut to size by a glass dealer. If, however, you require a mirror that is thin and light, plastic mirror may be the answer. Whatever mirrors you decide upon, they will have to be framed in the same way as were the pictures. A mirror in a room furnished with antiques would require a gilded metal or a carved wooden frame with perhaps an elaborate crest incorporated in the carving.

Mirrors for bathrooms look best unframed.

Clocks

Most of us have kept old wristwatches that gave up service years before. These make perfect wall clocks for dollhouses if the band fittings are removed. If you have no real watches, very good copies can easily be made. For the faces you will need a watch catalogue which are usually available free at department stores.

Wall Clocks

Cut out a clear picture of the style you prefer. Cut a piece of 4.8 mm balsa and shape it to suit the picture. Paint it, and glue the balsa and picture together (Fig. 101a).

Dressing Table Clocks

Make these the same way as pictures in frames are made. Glue a dial into an attractive metal frame that can be provided by a tiny brooch, ring setting, or even an old wristwatch case that has lost its works (Fig. 101b). To help them stand up, glue a small wooden support at the back and paint it to match the frame. If using a wristwatch case and the bar that once held the strap is still present, simply bend the bar back and the watchcase will stand very well on its own.

Fig. 101b
Dressing table clocks

Pocket Watch

Cut a circle about 6 mm diameter from 1.6 mm balsa. Paint it gold and add a tiny face cut from a catalogue. Attach a piece of fine jewellery chain to the top, and it is ready to drape across grandfather doll's waistcoat (Fig. 101c).

Fig. 101c
Pocket watch

Alarm Clocks

These need plain round faces. Cut a circle of 6.4 mm balsa, glue the face on it, glue a silver-painted domed bead on top for a bell, and make three little feet for it to stand on from beads or short lengths of toothpick (Fig. 101d).

Books

Obtain a coloured catalogue from a bookshop and choose some pictures of books showing clear, whole front covers. Cut them out, and also cut out the titles that are usually listed separately nearby. Sizes should not be more than approximately 35 mm × 30 mm for children's books, and 25 mm × 20 mm for other books. Vary their shapes a little. Also obtain a packet of kindergarten craft papers in various colours.

Books Made from Wood

To make these books, you will need a picture of a front cover of a book; the separate title to put on the spine; 4.8 mm balsa cut to the same size as the picture; and coloured craft paper to tone with the picture.

1. Cut the craft paper the same height as the picture and 1½ times its width.
2. Spread white glue on the craft paper and smooth the paper over the back of the balsa, around one edge (Fig. 102a).
3. Glue the picture over the front of the balsa, smoothing it carefully to the edges. Glue the separate title on to the spine — this may have to be abbreviated to fit on (Fig. 102b).
4. When the glue is quite dry, take a needle and scratch downwards on the exposed edge of the wood to separate the 'pages' (Fig. 102c).

Wood may also be covered with fine glove leather and embossed with gold. The family Bible looks impressive made this way, especially if a marker is used. To do this, use a craft knife to cut a slit in the bottom exposed edge of the book and insert (with a spot of glue) a tiny leather marker. 12 mm balsa makes a good-sized Bible or encyclopaedia, with the spine curved outwards and the front edges slightly curved inwards. Achieve this by rubbing the balsa gently with sandpaper before covering (Fig. 102d).

Fig. 101a
Wall clocks

Fig. 101d
Alarm clock

Books Made from Used Cheque Book Butts

Cut the cheque book across so that only 20 mm of the bound stapled end is left. Cut this end into 20 mm pieces. Each one forms a tiny book. Glue a picture and title on the cover (Fig. 103).

Books Made from Paper

1. Cut about 10 pieces of paper (bond typing paper is suitable) to 40 mm × 25 mm.
2. Cut one piece of thin smooth cardboard to 40 mm × 31 mm.
3. Lay the papers one on top of the other with the cardboard at the bottom, and machine stitch down the exact centre, starting and ending with a backstitch (Fig. 104a).

4. Fold the book closed and hammer it to fold and flatten it.
5. Cover the book with craft paper, then glue the first and last pages to the inside of the covers.
6. These little books can be used for your own recipes, music, short stories and so on. Print in the title on the front and glue on a suitable picture (Fig. 104b).

Larger versions of these paper books become scrapbooks, magazines or family albums. For albums use fawn-coloured pastel paper for the pages and glue in miniature pictures of people and places. Don't forget to print a title under each, even if you only manage a suggestion of printing because of the microscopic size (Fig. 104c).

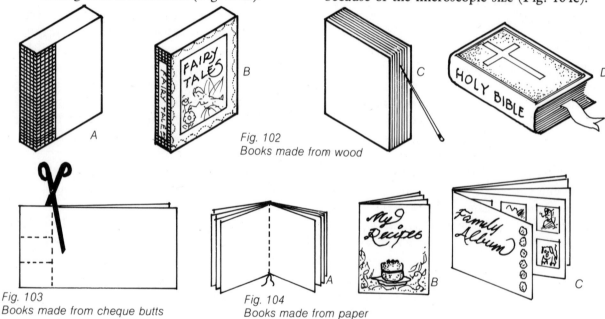

Fig. 102
Books made from wood

Fig. 103
Books made from cheque butts

Fig. 104
Books made from paper

Using Pictures from Advertisements

Groceries

Cut out the picture of the item you wish to make, then cut some balsa the size of the picture. Use 6.4 mm or 12.8 mm balsa for breakfast foods, soap powders, potato chips, packets of cheese, packets of biscuits, pet foods and so on. The areas of the wood not covered by the label should be painted or covered with craft paper of a matching colour.

Use 12 mm dowelling for round items such as tins of fruit, juices and soups.

When making tinned products, colour the bare wood top and bottom of the tin with a silver pen to simulate aluminium.

Blocks of Chocolate

Use silver foil over small squares of 3.2 mm balsa. Glue the labels on both the front and the back, allowing the silver to show around the sides.

Cosmetics

Soaps and toothpastes are made the same way as the groceries. Tins of talc are made of dowel with a fancy bead on the top.

Boxed Games

Use 3 mm balsa, cover with a suitable picture of snakes and ladders, chess, jigsaws or similar games, and suggest that this is a box either by having the bottom a different colour or by running a black pen line around the sides for a lid.

Bathroom Scales

Find a clear picture of the face of a set of scales and glue it on to 6.4 mm balsa that has been cut to shape and painted.

Wall Barometer

Make this in the same way as the scales, but use 3.2 mm balsa.

Knitting Wools

Loosely roll a tiny skein of wool and glue the end to prevent it coming apart. Look for an advertisement with a skein of wool, cut out the label, and glue it around the wool in a band.

Articles Made with Modelling Plastic

Purchase a packet of white modelling plastic from a craft shop and follow the instructions for the oven processing time. When joining two pieces together, use a smear of water to assist adhesion. Paint the completed articles with oil or acrylic paint.

Pipe for Grandfather Doll

Roll the plastic into a ball shape about 6 mm diameter. With the point of a pencil, depress the top to form a hole. Make a stem, join it to the bowl firmly, then give it a slight curve. After processing in the oven, paint it brown.

Mouse

Form a pear-shape about 12 mm or so long. Pinch in slightly near the narrow end to define the head. Press the article down to flatten it where it meets the table. Roll out a long thin tail and attach it to the mouse, then twist it into an S-shape. After processing, paint it pale brown and mark in two eyes with a black pen.

Parrot for a Cage

Form a fat sausage-shape about 20 mm long. Depress around the neck area to make the head, then gently shape the body, tapering down to the tail. After processing, colour it red with blue wings and black eyes (Fig. 105).

Eggs

Roll tiny pieces of modelling plastic into egg-shapes about 5 mm long. These do not require painting after processing. They can be placed into a little bowl and glued into position, or turned into Easter eggs by wrapping in coloured foil.

Pumpkin

Make a rough ball about 20 mm diameter. Indent with grooves like those of a real pumpkin and add a short thick stalk to the top. Cut out several wedges of the pumpkin with a sharp knife and use the point of a needle to make tiny marks to suggest seeds. After processing, paint the inside and wedges orange, the seeds darker orange, and the outside skin grey-green (Fig. 106).

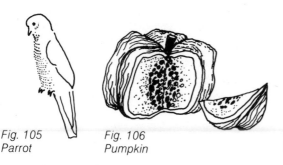

Fig. 105
Parrot

Fig. 106
Pumpkin

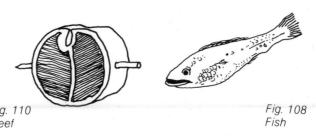

Fig. 110
Beef

Fig. 108
Fish

Carrots

Form a number of sausage-shapes about 20 mm long and roll thin at one end. Vary the lengths and shapes a little and curve some of the tails slightly. When processed, paint orange with a green or brown spot at the thick end.

Potatoes

Roll each one into a rough ball-shape 10 mm diameter. When processed, paint brown and before the paint is dry rub off a few spots here and there to look more natural.

Oranges

Shape each one into a ball about 10 mm diameter then roll it gently on a piece of rough sandpaper to give it the correct grain. When processed, paint orange.

Pears

Roll each one into a pear-shape 10 mm long and pinch out a tiny stalk at the narrow end. When processed, paint yellow with a few faint green marks here and there.

Bananas

Form a sausage-shape about 20 mm long, thin out slightly each end and curve a little. When processed, paint yellow with a few black streaky marks lengthwise and a black spot at each end.

Apples

Shape each one into a ball about 10 mm diameter and indent very slightly in one spot. When processed, paint bright red (or yellow-green if a cooking apple) and mark in a brown spot at the indent.

Box of Strawberries

Roll about a dozen pear-shapes 4 mm diameter. When processed, paint bright red with tiny black dots here and there and a green spot at the wide end. Following the directions given for making the tea tray, make a box just big enough to fit the strawberries in. Glue them into place.

Toffee Apples

Shape each one into a ball about 10 mm diameter. Cut 20 mm lengths from the pointed ends of toothpicks and insert into the apples. After processing, paint the apples bright red. If they are for dollhouse use, stand them in a plate, apple end down. If they are to be for sale in a dollshop, make a display tray for them by cutting 25 mm × 25 mm of 6.4 mm balsa, painting it, and drilling tiny holes for the sticks of the apples to stand in.

Ice-Cream Cones

Roll the plastic into 12 mm balls and drag down to a fine point to form the cone, but at the same time keep the head smooth and round. Mark a line of division between the cone and the ice-cream. When processed, paint the cones pale brown and the ice-cream white, pink, dark brown or any other suitable colour (Fig. 107).

Fish

Form a sausage-shape 25 mm long, flatten it, and pinch it into the shape of a fish. Press in some scale and tail marks with a needle point. Roll a tiny ball and add for each eye. When processed, paint the body silver and the eye red (Fig. 108).

Leg of Lamb

Roll a ball 20 mm diameter, flatten it on to the table and pull it long enough to form a shank. Make a few marks at the full end to suggest the bone. When processed, very slightly smear a little red paint on the outside so that it becomes streaky pink. Leave the 'bone' unpainted at the full end but paint around it with red (Fig. 109).

Fig. 109
Lamb

Fig. 107
Cones

Fig. 111
Sausages

Roasting Beef

Make a thin strip of plastic 60 mm × 10 mm. Roll it up and push a toothpick through for a skewer, allowing 3 mm to protrude at each end. When processed, streak the outside with a smear of red paint, leaving the rest of the beef unpainted except for some red painted in a circular direction on the two sides to indicate the rolled meat (Fig. 110).

Minced Steak

Flatten out a rough shape about 20 mm × 15 mm × 5 mm thick. Chop it all over with a ballpoint pen that has the point retracted. When processed, paint it red and, while the paint is still wet, rub some of the paint off with a rag.

Lamb Chops

Roll some balls about 10 mm and flatten into ovals 5 mm thick. With a needle point, make marks to divide the meat area from the fat (look at a real chop for guidance). When processed, paint the meat red and leave the fat unpainted.

Sausages

Form thin sausage-shapes 20 mm long, tapering at the ends. Leave some as separate sausages and pile the rest into small heaps (with a smear of water for adherence), then process. They will not need painting (Fig. 111).

Cooked Tomatoes

Roll balls 6 mm diameter and cut them in halves or quarters with a sharp knife. When processed, paint red with touches of green for seeds.

Cooked Green Peas

Roll tiny balls about 2 mm diameter. When processed, paint pale green and, while the paint is wet, bunch about 12 or so together in heaps.

Potato Chips

These can be made by rolling the plastic flat and slicing it into miniature strips, then processing. Leave unpainted. However they may also be made by slicing 3.2 mm balsa into 10 mm × 2 mm pieces and painting them pale yellow.

Cooked Carrots

Form carrot shapes as previously directed, then cut in quarters. When processed, paint orange.

Cooked Spaghetti

Put a piece of modelling plastic in a garlic press — and spaghetti will be the result! Pile it into small heaps, 12–15 mm diameter. When processed, paint pale yellow.

Fig. 112
Chop and vegetables

Fig. 113
Pie and vegetables

Fig. 114
Sausages and egg

Fig. 115
Fish and chips

Fig. 116
Sandwiches

A Plate of Chop and Vegetables

Follow the instructions for making the lamb chops but, after processing, paint them brown, keeping a little of the 'fat' unpainted. Put a chop on a miniature plate and add a selection of cooked vegetables. Glue them all into position (Fig. 112).

A Plate of Meat Pie and Vegetables

Roll a ball of modelling plastic about 10 mm diameter and flatten it top and bottom. Press a crimped edge all around with a needle. Make a few score marks on the top with a knife. When processed, paint pale brown. Put the pie on a miniature plate, add some cooked vegetables, and glue them all into place (Fig. 113).

A Plate of Sausages and Eggs

Follow the instructions for making sausages but, after processing, paint them brown. To make the eggs, flatten some plastic into 10 mm circles. On top of each, place a ball 3 mm diameter and flatten it (have a smear of water in between). When processed, paint the inside circle yellow and the outside one white. Place sausages and eggs on a miniature plate — add a tomato if you wish for colour — and glue into position (Fig. 114).

A Plate of Fish and Chips

Follow the instructions for making the fish but, after processing, paint it pale brown, including the eye. Place the fish on a miniature plate, add some potato chips and glue into position (Fig. 115).

A Plate of Sandwiches

Using a piece of dowel as a rolling pin, roll out some plastic 2 mm thick. Cut this into three 15 mm squares with a sharp knife. Carefully lift the squares with the blade of the knife and place them one on top of the other, smearing a little water in between. With the point of a needle, roughen the visible edges of the centre square to simulate the sandwich filling, allowing small pieces to protrude. Mark the top square into four sections as a real sandwich would be cut. When processed, paint the filling brown, red and green (for, say, meat, tomato and lettuce). Glue the sandwich on to a miniature plate (Fig. 116).

Scones on a Baking Tray

The tray: Select a piece of unpainted aluminium from a used drink can, cut it to 25 mm × 28 mm and flatten it with a hammer. With plyers turn up the edges about 1.5 mm all around.
The scones: Flatten some modelling plastic to 5 mm and cut it into rounds with a pastry cutter. When processed, glue the scones on to the tray and paint the tops a pale brown.
The pastry cutter: Snip a short end off a large plastic drinking straw.

Pastry on a Board

Pastry board: Cut about 35 mm × 25 mm from 3.2 mm balsa. Press the point of a needle around the top edges for a fancy appearance.
Rolling pin: Cut a 30 mm length from 6 mm dowel. Shape small handles at the ends with a craft knife, and sandpaper.
Pastry: Using a piece of dowel, roll out plastic to 2 mm thick in an uneven shape 30 mm × 20 mm in size. Cut out a few holes with a pastry cutter. Process the pastry. Do not paint it.

Glue the pastry on to the board, and the rolling pin on top (Fig. 117).

Donuts

Roll a ball and flatten it to a circle 10 mm diameter. Cut a hole from the centre with the pastry cutter. When processed, paint pale brown.

Gingerbread Men

Roll out some plastic and shape figures 20 mm long. Make some tiny balls and press on for buttons. When processed, paint the figure brown with black buttons. Add black eyes and a red smiling mouth with felt pens (Fig. 118).

Fruit Cake

Shape plastic to an oblong 20 mm × 15 mm × 15 mm. Make small indentations all over with the end of a ballpoint pen. With a sharp knife cut off two or three slices. Indent the newly cut areas. When processed, paint pale brown all over. When the paint is dry, spot all the cake roughly with a black felt pen to represent sultanas, and spot here and there with a red pen for cherries (Fig. 119).

Iced Cherry Cake

Make a round shape 20 mm diameter × 15 mm high and flatten the bottom. Pat the sides straight. Make a tiny ball and place on the top for the cherry. When processed, paint the cake brown and allow to dry. Then paint the top pink and let the paint run unevenly down the sides as in the illustration. Paint the cherry red (Fig. 120).

Iced Cup Cakes

Make in the same way as the cherry cake but on a much smaller scale — say 8 mm diameter. Add a cherry to the top or a circle of decorations around the edge. When processed, paint them pink or brown or white (Fig. 121).

Chocolate Cream Cake

Make a round shape 20 mm across and 15 mm high, and flatten the bottom. Pat the sides straight. Roll a very thin sausage of plastic and with a smear of water attach it around the cake like a belt, pressing it in slightly. Put a little ball on top for a cherry or nut. When processed, paint the cake dark brown except for the rolled strip which can be painted white. Paint the decoration on the top (Fig. 122).

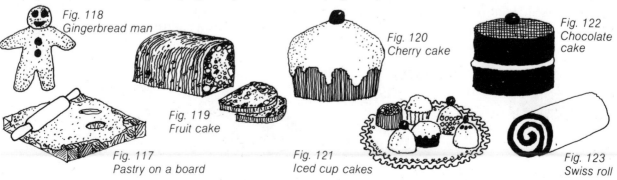

Fig. 118
Gingerbread man

Fig. 119
Fruit cake

Fig. 117
Pastry on a board

Fig. 120
Cherry cake

Fig. 122
Chocolate cake

Fig. 121
Iced cup cakes

Fig. 123
Swiss roll

Swiss Roll

Roll out some plastic to 2 mm thick and cut an oblong 70 mm × 20 mm. Roll up firmly. When processed, paint the outside very pale brown, leaving the ends of the roll unpainted. With red paint fill in the indentations of the roll to represent jam (Fig. 123).

Fruit Pie

Excellent pie plates can be made from small round recessed finger pulls (used on sliding doors and available at hardware stores). To make a pie, fill the pie plate with modelling plastic. Roll out a top 'pie crust' and cover the pie. Cut out a generous slice with a sharp pointed knife. With a needle, roughen the 'fruit' in the pie, being careful not to disturb the crust. Use the needle to crimp a pattern around the edge of the pie. When processed, paint the inside fruit red and the crust pale brown (Fig. 124).

Strawberry Tart

The most impressive tart plates are the crimped tops found on beer bottles. Roll out some modelling plastic and line the tart plate. Make some tiny balls of plastic and fill the tart closely. When processed, paint the strawberries red. Leave the tart edge unpainted. Remove the tart from the plate. If you wish, cut the tart into slices before processing in the oven (Fig. 125).

Jam Tart

Roll out plastic and line a tart plate. Fill the tart with plastic but keep it 2 mm below the level of the top and roughen it with a needle. Make some very thin narrow strips of plastic for the pastry strips and lay them over the tart in a lattice pattern. When processed, paint the 'jam' red but leave the pastry edge and strips unpainted (Fig. 126).

Pineapple Meringue Tart

Make this in the same way as the strawberry tart but paint the filling yellow. When the paint is dry, put a teaspoon of plaster of paris in a small tin and add enough water to make it sloppy but not too wet. Work very quickly or it will set. With a toothpick, pile small heaps of plaster on to the pie and stir each into a meringue-like whirl. Allow to set (Fig. 127).

Loaf of Bread

Make an oblong 30 mm × 15 mm × 15 mm. Round off the top slightly. With a knife, indent halfway along the top to form the loaf division. When processed, paint pale brown with a darker brown on the top.

Fancy bread is made in the same way but a little smaller and without the division. Slash marks along the top diagonally, or add a plait or twist running lengthwise.

Sliced Bread with Knife and Breadboard

Sliced bread: Make a loaf of bread as suggested, then with a sharp knife cut about three thin slices from one end. Allow these to stay in a heap naturally as they fall. After processing, paint the loaf as suggested, including the crust around the slices, but be careful not to get any paint on the cut surfaces of the bread.

Breadboard: Cut about 35 mm × 20 mm from 3.2 mm balsa. Decorate the edges with a needle.

Bread knife: Roll a thin sausage-shape of plastic about 15 mm long × 3 mm diameter to form the handle. For the blade cut a piece of the aluminium serrated edge from a box of plastic wrap and carefully cut out a tiny blade 15 mm long × 4 mm wide including the serrated edge. Insert one end of the blade into the end of the handle and press together slightly. Process in the oven, then paint the handle a bright colour.

Glue the bread and the heap of slices on to the breadboard and stand the knife in the cutting position (Fig. 128).

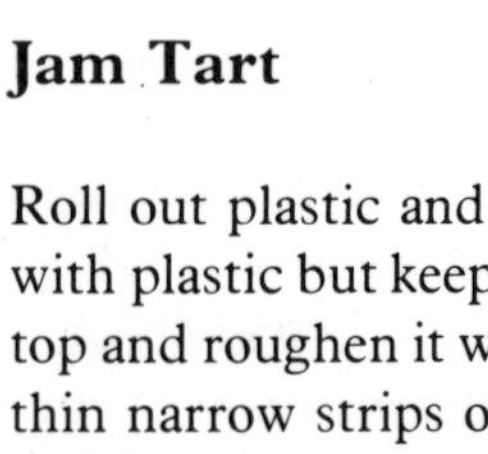

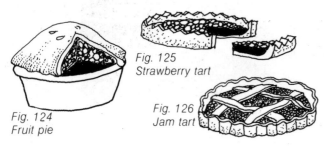

Fig. 124
Fruit pie

Fig. 125
Strawberry tart

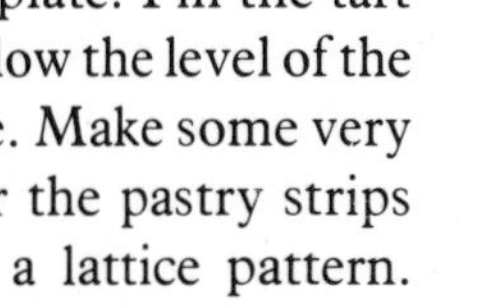

Fig. 126
Jam tart

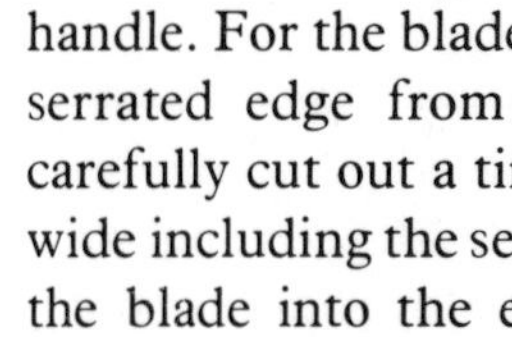

Fig. 127
Meringue tart

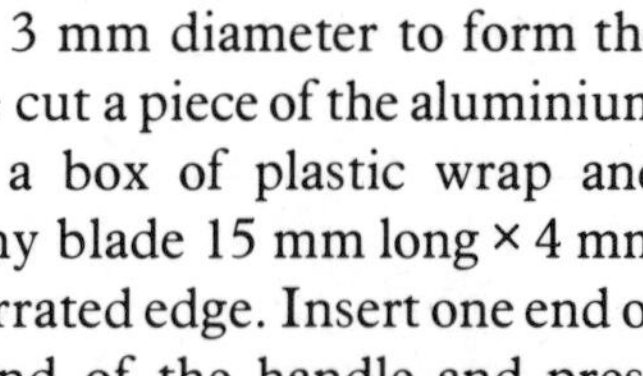

Fig. 128
Sliced bread

Making Food from Dough

Make a dough of one cup of plain flour and one cup of salt mixed together and moistened with water to a dryish consistency. Knead it until smooth and stiff and able to hold its shape. This can now be formed into loaves of bread and bread rolls. Poppy seeds may be added to the tops if wished. Cakes can also be made from the mixture, with food colouring added when required.

Jam Tart

Line a tart plate with pastry, paint inside the tart with cochineal, and lattice over this with narrow strips of dough.

Fruit Pie

Line a tart plate with thin pastry, fill this with some very tiny pieces of pastry rolled into balls and coloured, then add the top layer of pastry. Trim the edges and press around the rim with a toothpick to decorate. With a sharp pointed knife, cut out a generous slice to expose the inside of the pie.

Cooking the Foods Made with Dough

Brush a little water over the tops and place all the foods on a scone tray. Cook in a moderate oven until they are golden brown — because of the tiny sizes involved they will require watching in case they burn.

When making foods with dough, remember that they will rise. Allowance will have to be made for this when forming them, otherwise they will be out of proportion for the dollhouse.

Making Food from Other Materials

Custard Tart

Roll out modelling plastic thinly and line a tart plate. When processed, mix some plaster of paris (have it wet enough to pour but not too liquid) and add a few drops of yellow paint or food colour. Spoon it quickly into the 'pastry' case and sprinkle with nutmeg. When the 'custard' has set, remove the tart from the plate.

Fig. 129
Chocolate pudding with custard

Fig. 130
Ice-cream with sauce

Chocolate Pudding and Custard

You will need four miniature dessert dishes for this recipe.

Using modelling plastic, make a round shape 15 mm diameter × 5 mm high. Cut it into four wedges. When processed, paint them dark brown and allow to dry. Place a wedge in each dessert dish. Mix some plaster of paris just wet enough to pour, tint yellow, and quickly spoon it around the chocolate pudding — but not over the top of it. Allow it to set (Fig. 129).

Fig. 131
Milkshake

Fig. 132
Wedding cake

Glasses of Wine

Have some miniature plastic glasses ready. Mix a few drops of cochineal with a little clear varnish and quickly pour into the glasses. Allow to set.

A Jug of Cream

Have a miniature jug ready. Mix a little wet but not liquid plaster of paris and quickly spoon it into the jug. Immediately insert a tiny spoon. With a toothpick, swirl the top of the 'cream' and allow it to set.

Flour

Use talcum powder rather than real flour if you are using it on a pastry board or standing some in a cannister. Talcum lasts longer and does not attract insects.

Wedding Cake

Cut out 1 circle 30 mm diameter × 12.8 mm balsa; 1 circle 20 mm diameter × 12.8 mm balsa; and 1 circle 12 mm diameter × 6.4 mm balsa.

Glue one on top of the other in a tier. Glue guipure lace flowers around the outside edges and the top surfaces. Paint it all over with undercoat, then a coat of white paint. Glue a tiny pearl bead on the centre top. Cut a circle 35 mm diameter from the centre of a paper doily and glue it under the wedding cake (Fig. 132).

Milkshakes

You will need some miniature plastic parfait glasses or tumblers for this recipe.

Prepare the following ingredients before starting the milkshakes as you will have to work very quickly. Put a little plaster of paris into an egg cup. Add one drop of cochineal then as many drops of water as are needed to make the mixture wet but not too liquid. Spoon it into the glasses to three-quarters full. Quickly sprinkle each one with a very tiny pinch of bicarbonate of soda and immediately insert a 'straw' made of white-painted rigid wire. Allow to set before moving (Fig. 131).

Ice-Cream with Strawberry Sauce

You will need four miniature dessert dishes for this recipe.

Using modelling plastic, make four balls no more than 10 mm diameter and process them. Paint them white and allow to dry. Place a ball of ice-cream in each dish. In a small tin mix a little clear varnish with a few drops of cochineal and pour around — not over — the ice-cream. Allow to set (Fig. 130).

Stew in a Saucepan

Chop up some fragments of balsa and put them into a miniature saucepan. Pour a little brown paint over, covering all the wood, and allow to dry.

Other Ideas

If you have finished your first dollhouse why not make another one? Perhaps next time you could try something different.

Why not a little 'street' of shops? Each shop could be made from the basic unit (Fig. 1). Add a counter and shelves for the stock, and print the name of the business on the front. Fire, ambulance and service stations could be made in the same way. If each roof is left flat the shops may be stacked and stored away quite easily.

A terrace of Victorian-style houses (Fig. 3) is another possibility.

If you are interested in theatre you could find the making of a miniature theatre a rewarding enterprise. It would need to be wide enough to allow at least several children to see the stage at the same time. A few rows of seats must be provided for the audience who would no doubt come along from the local dollhouses. Cover the inside surfaces of the front doors with photos of ballet, opera and theatre stars and advertisements of coming events. Include a painted-on box office and an admissions price. Paint the ceiling dark blue and glue on some gold stars, paint the walls with people sitting in boxes, make a small orchestra pit and add some stage curtains. A side door opening on to the stage would allow discreet changes of actors, and the operation by drawstring of the stage curtains. A change of backdrops could be made through a slot above the stage. A small light over the stage area would be essential. The scenery and cardboard actors (which you would naturally make yourself) could be stored in the attic roof. In the roof also could be placed a cassette player with tapes to provide voices for the stage presentation. Write and record your own plays, not forgetting to provide suitable music for the intervals.

Very young children would appreciate a zoo to play with. Make it on a solid flat board. Design pathways curling around among fenced-in enclosures. Have a bridge crossing over a pond of ducks or crocodiles. Blue water is simulated by painting beneath clear perspex. Glue on small stones for the rocks, and where there are arctic animals paint the rocks white. Add trees, flower-beds and grass. Make an icecream kiosk and perhaps a see-saw, or a pony to give rides. Do not forget to put feed boxes filled with grass in the enclosures for the animals.

You will probably have many more ideas of your own. Whatever you make you can be quite sure it will be thoroughly enjoyed by its recipient. Happy memories are usually made in childhood, and for your own loved ones you have it in your hands to make them something that is worth remembering.

Index

Bathroom scales 69
Beds, antique 53
    bassinet 54
    cot 54
    cradle 54
    modern 53
Bedside table 46
Blinds, painted 11
    roller 16
Blossom Cottage 39
Bolts of fabric 62
Book case 46
    shelves 46
Books made from cheque butts 68
    from paper 68
    from wood 67
Bottles 65
Bread making 74
    sliced 74
Brickwork, simulated 9
Broom 61

Cage for parrot 60
Cake, chocolate cream 73
    fruit 73
    iced cherry 73
    iced cup 73
    swiss roll 74
    wedding 75, 76
Candle holders 63
Cannisters 63
Chair, dining 48
    kitchen 48
    lounge 49
    nursery 47
Chocolate pudding 75
Chocolates 68
Christmas tree 60
Clocks, alarm 67
    dressing table 67
    learning the time 59
    wall 67
Clothes for female dolls 25
    little boy dolls 33
    little girl dolls 32
    male dolls 32
Coathangers 64
Colour schemes 9, 13
Cosmetics 68

Counting beads 59
Curtains 16

Dollhouse building 4
    buying 2
    designing 4
Dolls, buying 20
    making 21
    toy baby 58
    toy pram 58
Donuts 73
Door, cut-out 10
    designs for 4
    painted-on 11
Dressing table 55
Dressmaker's model 60
Duster 61

Eggs 69

Fire 53
Fireplace 52
Floor coverings 13
Flour 76
Foods made from dough 75
    modelling plastic 69
    other materials 75
Footstool 56
Furniture buying 15
    making 15
Fish 70
Flower making 64
    vases 64
Frames for pictures 66
Fruit 70

Games 69
Gift cards 62
Gingerbread men 73
Groceries 68

Hairstyles for dolls 24
Horse rocker 57

Icecream cones 76

Jug of cream 76

Kitchen dresser 47

Knitting wools 69

Letter racks 62
Letters 62
Lightfittings, buying 14
     making 14
Linen press 46
Linley Court 36

Manchester 16
Matches 63
Materials for making accessories 18
     dollhouses 4
     furniture 15
Meat 69, 70, 71, 72
Milk shakes 76
Mirrors 66
Modelling plastic dollheads 21
    foods 19
    various 69
Mop 61
Mouse 69

Nameplates 12

Ornamental busts 64

Painting and decorating 9
Paints 9
Paper patterns 62
Parrot 69
Pastry 73
Patterns for clothes 35
Pictures for frames 66
Pies 72, 75
Pipe 69
Pots for plants 64
Pram toy 58

Quoits 58

Rainbow Arcade 42
Residents 20

Room sizes 4

Sandwiches 72
Schoolhouse 41
Scones 73
Shingle tiles 9
Sideboard 47
Spaghetti 71
Spike file 62
Stairs 7
Statues 64
Stew in saucepans 76

Table, dining 51
   kitchen 50
   nursery 50
   occasional 51
Taps 63
Tarts, custard 75
   jam 74
   made from dough 75
   pineapple meringue 74
   strawberry 74
Tea tray 63
Television set 56
Train, toy 59

Umbrella 61

Vanity stool 56
   table 56
Vases 64
Vegetables 70

Walking stick 61
Wall barometer 69
Wallpapers 13
Wallshelf 57
Wardrobe 47
Window shutters 12
Windows, cut-out 10
    painted-on 11